THE PAPERS

OF

Col. Richard H. Gilliam

OF

BUCKINGHAM COUNTY, VIRGINIA

Carl C. Rosen

HERITAGE BOOKS
2025

HERITAGE BOOKS

AN IMPRINT OF HERITAGE BOOKS, INC.

Books, CDs, and more—Worldwide

For our listing of thousands of titles see our website
at
www.HeritageBooks.com

A Facsimile Reprint
Published 2025 by
HERITAGE BOOKS, INC.
Publishing Division
5810 Ruatan Street
Berwyn Heights, MD 20740

Previously published
1992

International Standard Book Number
Paperbound: 978-1-58549-218-3

DEDICATED TO

My wife, Virginia Elcan Rosen

and

Margaret Elcan Taylor

Sisters and great-granddaughters

of Colonel R.H. Gilliam

Richard Holland Gilliam (1809 - 1892)
Courtesy of Richard H. Gilliam, Jr., great-grandson of Col. Gilliam

Courthouse and Clerks Office

FIRE OF 24TH FEBRUARY 1869

At a court continued and held for Buckingham County in the Brick Tavern House occupied by John M. **Hooper** on Thursday the 11th day of March 1869.

Whereas the courthouse and clerks office of this county were consumed by fire on the night of the 24th of February last and now it being the duty of this court to provide a courthouse and clerks office for the county- with a view to use speedy performance of this duty the court doeth appoint N. F. **Bocock** and William **Hocker** in district No 1, William R. **Wright** and Chapman **Glover** in district No 2, Geo D. **Saunders** and Rich H. **Gilliam** in district No 3, Edmund W. **Hubard** and William E. **Gannaway** in district No 4, James B. **Ficklin** & D. J. **Woodfin** in district No 5, and Henry St. Geo **Harris** and Jno C. **Turner** in district No 6, commissioners whose duty it shall be to obtain prepare and report to the court as soon as practicable such plans for a courthouse and clerks office as they may deem suitable of the court, and the court doth further empower said comrs or any two of them to take such steps as may seem necessary to them to preserve and secure from work and material of the old courthouse building and enclosure now remaining. And the court doth further direct that a copy of this order be forthwith served by the Sheriff of this county on each one of the commissioners approved.

A copy teste

R. K. **Irving**

CONTENTS

Portrait of Richard Holland Gilliam (1809-1892) v

Appointment of commissioners for the planning of new courthouse and clerks office vi

Introduction ix

Orders to Summons 1

Orders to Sell Property 1

Adjudged Debts and Court Charges, Circa 1841 7

Promissory Notes and Receipts 23

Bonds, Notes, Loans, Receipts 33

Sale of property of Samuel Gregory (deceased) 36

Hardiman Estate 38

Militia Fines 39

List of Tickets to be Collected 40

Poor House of Buckingham County 40

Schools (Teachers, School Taxes, Tuition), ... 43

Tax Assessments 45

Ticket Lists 50

Accounts: 54
    Horses, carriages, gigs, wagons 54
    Coffins and burial articles 55
    Shoes 55
    Tailoring 56
    Tanning hides 56
    Sawmills and lumber 57
    Medical and dental bills 57
    Roads, tolls 58
    Hotel and tavern bills 59
    Subscriptions 59
    Mercantile 60
Partnership of Joel G. Brown and Richard H. Gilliam 60

List of Merchants from the Gilliam Papers 61

Escape of Alfred Childers 62

Sheriffalty 63

Letter from J. H. French 63

Apprenticeship of Richard Gilliam to Coach Painting, Trimming 64

Abstract of Will of Richard Gilliam (1760-1839) 65

Genealogical Chart of the Gilliam Family - The First Six Generations 66

The Gilliam Family 67

Index 81

INTRODUCTION

The data contained in this publication are based on the personal letters, documents, and sheriff receipt book of Colonel Richard Holland Gilliam. Some of the papers are personal in nature; most relate to his activities as Deputy Sheriff of Buckingham County.

As Deputy Sheriff of Buckingham County, Colonel Gilliam (as he was called) executed many of the functions assigned to the sheriff's office. His duties included the serving of papers from the county court and the execution of other actions of the county government including the collection of fines, taxes, court claims and other debts. The great importance of these papers largely stems from their being the only source of information on certain activities of the county government prior to the courthouse fire of 1869. These papers date from 1825 to 1870. We hope the publication of them will help those involved in historical and genealogical research of Buckingham County.

Apparently Colonel Gilliam, like many of that time, saved virtually every scrap of paper. His papers were stored in a very old tomato box with the name of the town of Ca Ira (Cumberland County) stencilled on one end. The receipt book is made of leather; a photograph of it is shown on the cover. These records had been saved through the years by his family. The author found them stored in Elk Hurst, Buckingham County, at the home built by George Hannah Elcan, Sr. Mrs. Elcan, the former Margaret Virginia Gilliam, was the granddaughter of Colonel R. H. Gilliam. The family once considered burning the papers; fortunately this didn't happen.

This book consists chiefly of abstracts of selected papers of the Gilliam Collection. Much of the legal wording has been eliminated and changed for ease in reading. Minor corrections have been made to spelling. Certain spellings and wording have been retained. Some of the papers have been re-arranged for purposes of clarity. On page 54 appear abstracts of several accounts of Colonel Gilliam. I chose not to reproduce these many records in their entirety in order to keep the size of this work within bounds.

For those interested in more information on Colonel Gilliam and his family we have added a final section which gives a brief genealogy of his ancestry and many of his descendants. I am indebted to several members of the family for their assistance in compiling this material.

Carl C. Rosen
Westminster, Maryland,1992

ABBREVIATIONS

Meanings of some of the less obvious abbreviations used in the papers as interpreted by the compiler.

a/c = account(s)

acct. = account

adm = administrator

agnst = against

assee = assignee

bbls = barrels

clk = clerk

cr = creditor

decd, dec'd = deceased

dr = debtor, doctor

dy = delivery [bond]

est = estate

ex, exr, excr, exor = executor

grd., gdn = guardian

med = medicine

pltfs = plaintiffs

pr. = pair

qr. = quart

sd. = said

shff = sheriff

ORDERS TO SUMMONS
(In file marked "Court Forms.")

1. Orders to the sheriff, commanding him to summons John AUSTIN, Bernard AUSTIN, Grace R. AUSTIN and Thomas AUSTIN to answer Bill in Chancery exhibited agnst them by William H. WORD & Quinn, M. WORD, late merchants and partners trading under the style and firm of William H. WORD & Co. 23 Dec 1841

2. Order to sheriff to summons Grace R. AUSTIN in her own right & as executrix of Archid. AUSTIN, dec'd., James M. AUSTIN in his own right and as excr. of A. AUSTIN, dec'd, Thomas AUSTIN in his own right and as exor. of A. AUSTIN, dec'd., Wm. M. MOSELEY, Bernard AUSTIN, Archibald AUSTIN, John AUSTIN, George AUSTIN, Martha E. AUSTIN, Frances AUSTIN, Grace AUSTIN, the two last infants under 21 years, to answer a bill in chancery exhibited against them by David JOHNSON and Joseph E. MORGAN, late merchants who sue for David JOHNSON. 17 Dec 1846.

3. Order to sheriff to summons William M. THURMOND to satisfy James T. SMITH and John W. MOSBY, who sue for the benefit of John THOMPSON Jr. and Joseph K. IRVING to the extent of one moiety of the debt, the sum of $563.66 ... which they have recovered against said Wm. M. THURMOND for debt. 6 Jan 1843.

ORDERS TO SELL PROPERTY

Following are orders which allowed the sheriff to sell personal property to satisfy suits, debts and court costs. These were orders to the sheriff of Buckingham County, "that of the goods and chattels of _[Name of person]_ ..., you cause to be made ..." [in the recovery of judgements and debts, etc.]

1. Goods and chattels of Thomas W. ISBELL and William ISBELL - $428.88 which Thomas H. FLOOD and Bryant NOWLIN merchants and partners in trade under the firm & style of FLOOD & NOWLIN have recovered against said Thos. W. & William ISBELL (on a delivery bond forfeited plus $5.08 for court costs. 20 June 1843.

2. Goods and chattels of Archibald AUSTIN and Thomas AUSTIN - $73.46 which Wm. BRANCH & Wm. HOLMAN late merchants and partners who traded under the firm and style of BRANCH and HOLMAN who sue for the benefit of William BRANCH and have recovered against said Archd. AUSTIN and Thomas AUSTIN (as delivery bond) plus $5.08 for court costs. 9 Sep 1842.

3. Goods and chattels of Clifford CABELL and Davis W. CABELL - $862.78 which Ammon HANCOCK and Isaac ADAMS late partners trading under the style of HANCOCK & ADAMS have recovered against said CABELLs (on a forthcoming bond forfeited), plus court costs. 15 Nov 1844.

4. Goods and chattels of Lewis W. CABELL - $109.88 which Frederick G. PETERS surviving partner of himself and Willis H. WILLS, dec'd, late merchants and partners trading under the firm & style of PETERS & WILLS, plus court costs. 20 Nov 1843.

5. Goods and chattels of Benjamin S. MORRIS - $44.67 which Joseph BRIGHTWELL and Wm. C. FLOURNOY late merchants & partners in trade under the style of BRIGHTWELL & Co, plus court costs. 24 Aug 1843.

6. Goods and chattels of William W. FERGUSON and Robert RIVES, late merchants and partners under the firm of William W. FERGUSON &Co. - $18.67 which George WEBB, James M. WEBB, Philip WATKINS and Warner W. PRICE recovered against FERGUSON &Co. for their costs by them about their defence expended, in an injunction obtained against them by said FERGUSON &Co. 7 May 1844.

7. Goods and chattels of Lawson G. TYLER - $50 which Jos. MOSELEY and Edward B. MOSELEY and Nathan SPENCER later merchants & partners in trade under the firm and style of J & EB MOSELEY & Co. who sue for the benefit of F. N. WATKINS trustee &c., recovered against said Lawson G. TYLER. 20 Nov 1844.

8. Goods and chattels of Samuel S. LAYNE - $29.05 which Wilson P. BRYAN and William T. YOUNG merchants and partners trading under the style and firm of BRYANT and YOUNG, recovered against said LAYNE for debt. 7 Sep 1843.

9. Goods and chattels of Thomas W. ISBELL & William ISBELL - $665.84 which Henry D. FLOOD and Thomas TRENT late merchants and partners in trade under the firm of FLOOD & TRENT who sue for the benefit of Thomas TRENT, recovered against said Thos. W. & William ISBELL (on a delivery bond forfeited) plus court costs. 20 June 1843.

10. Goods and chattels of Benjamin S. MORRIS - $62.08 which Thomas S. MORTON and Charles A. MORTON, millers and partners in trade under the firm & style of Thos. S. & C. A. MORTON, recovered against said MORRIS as well for a certain debt as for interest thereon. 24 Aug 1843.

11. Goods and chattels of Lewis W. CABELL and Clifford CABELL - $481.34 which George G. CURL & Armstead LONG & Eliza. H. LONG his wife late Eliza: R. PERRY, which said Curl and Perry were late carpenters and partners doing business under the style and firm of George G. CURL &Co., recovered against said CABELLs (on a forthcoming bond forfeited) for debt. 9 Jan 1846.

12. Goods and chattels of John R. WADE and Wilson HIX - $189.74 which Silas P. VAWTER assee of James H. FARELEY, recovered against said WADE & HIX (on a delivery bond forfeited) plus court costs. 20 Jan 1845.

13. Goods and chattels of Benjamin MOSELEY and Richard H. GILLIAM - $286.64 which Waddy W. ROBERTS administrator of Zachariah ROBERTS, dec'd. ...1846.

14. Goods and chattels of Thomas W. ISBELL ... obliges of himself and George CHRISTIAN - $225 which Thomas H. FLOOD recovered against said Thos. W. ISBELL for debt. 23 Sep 1842

15. Goods and chattels of William HIX and James C. STEPHANS - $884.46 which James DUNLOP, Henry MONCUNE and Thomas W. McCANCE, merchants and partners trading under the style & firm of DUNLOP, MONCURE &Co. assignees of James M. RATCLIFFE on the common law side, have recovered against the said Wilson HIX and James C. STEPHENS for the penalty of a bond taken for the forthcoming of property at the day of sale. 6 March 1844.

16. Goods and chattels of B. T. MORRIS - $55 which Thomas B. WOOTTON who sues for the benefit of Tample D. RICKARDSON trustees,

recovered against said MORRIS as well for a certain debt as for interest thereon. 24 Aug 1843,

17. Goods and chattels of Charles PHELPS - $51.88 which Henry BIBB assignee of George W. BIBB recovered against said PHELPS. -- Nov 1843.

18. Goods and chattels of Samuel J. WALKER and John N. WEST - $4370.10, recovered against them. 29 Sep 1843.

19. Goods and chattels of Thomas W. ISBELL and William ISBELL - $7406, which William D. CHRISTIAN recovered against said ISBELLs (on a forthcoming bond forfeited. 12 Dec 1843.

20. Goods and chattels of Thomas W. ISBELL and William ISBELL - $341.40 which Cincinnatus F. JONES recovered against ISBELLs (on a delivery bond forfeited. 25 Sep 1843.

21. Goods and chattels of Lewis W. CABELL - $116.06 which John G. MEEM recovered against CABEL as well for a certain debt as for interest thereon. 9 Oct 1844.

22. Goods and chattels of Thomas W. ISBELL & William ISBELL - $387.40 which James ANDERSON recovered against said Thos. W. & William ISBELL (on a delivery bond forfeited. 20 June 1843.

23. Goods and chattels of Clifford CABELL and Lewis W. CABELL - $1512.82 which Benjamin W. S. CABELL for the benefit of E.W. & R. T. HUBARD transferees of George BOOKER recovered against the said CLIFFORD and Lewis W. CABELL on a motion on a forth coming bond forfeited. Also $3.56 for his costs in that behalf expended. We also command you that of the goods and chattels of the said Clifford CABELL you cause to be made $71.34 to which the said Ben W. T. CABELL for the sd. HUBARD is entitled for his damages by reason of the said Clifford CABELL's retarding the execution of the judgement aforesaid by an injunction. 24 May 1845.

24. Goods and chattels of S. P. HARDWICKE and D. O. BASS - $129.92 which John P. CALLAHAN who sues for the benefit of Elisha J. HUNDLEY, recovered against the said HARDWICKE and BASS on delivery bond forfeited. 19 Sep 1843.

25. Goods and chattels of Samuel P. HARDWICK, William F. BON-DURANT and John B. GARY - $114.94 which Samuel MORRIS styles administrator of James PITTMAN, dec'd who sues for the benefit of Samuel HATCHER, recovered against said HARDWICK &c. (on a delivery bond forfeited). 19 Aug 1845.

26. Goods and chattels of Clifford CABELL and Lewis W. CABELL - $298.76 which Jefferson D. TURNER recovered against said Cabells (on a forthcoming bond forfeited). 22 Sep 1845.

27. Goods and chattels of Thomas W. ISBELL and William ISBELL - $165.94 which William D. CHRISTIAN recovered against said Thomas W. & William ISBELL (on a dy bond forfeited). 16 Oct 1843.

28. Goods and chattels of Benjamin S. MORRIS - $33.31 which Josiah W. BRIGHTWELL administrator of Samuel CROXTON, dec'd, recovered against said MORRIS as well for a certain debt as for interest thereon. 24 Aug 1843.

29. Goods and chattels of Lewis W. CABELL and Clifford CABELL - $173.10 which Don. T. C. PETERS recovered against said CABELLs (on a forthcoming bond forfeited). 22 Sep 1845.

30. Goods and chattels of Robert MOORE, administrator of Mary WRIGHT, dec'd - $5.40 which Robert GLOVER recovered against him for costs expended in defending a certain action of de... by the said Robert MOORE admr as aforesaid against the said GLOVER lately ...? 12 June 1843.

31. Goods and chattels of J. S. ROBERTSON and M. C. OBRIANT - $60, which E. J. GILLIAM, guardian of John GARY's children recovered against said ROBERTSON and as well for a certain debt as for interest thereon. Nov 1845.

32. Goods and chattels of David W. GLOVER and N. D. MORRIS - $160.86 which James BROWN recovered against said Glover &c (on a forthcoming bond forfeited). 22 Sep 1845.

33. Goods and chattels of Charles COLEMAN and Henry COLEMAN and William H. PARRACK - $454.10 which Samuel J. WALKER, Samuel D.

McDEARMON and David C. JONES recovered against said COLEMANs &c. on a forthcoming bond forfeited. 21 Apr 1845.

34. Goods and chattels of Thomas W. ISBELL and William ISBELL - $409.30 which Lawrence ANDERSON recovered against said Thos. W. and William ISBELL (on a delivery bond forfeited). 20 June 1843.

35. Goods and chattels of Samuel P. HARDWICKE and William F. BON-DURANT - $152.90 which Laurence ANDERSON who sues for the benefit of James H. FORBES recovered against said HARDWICK &c. (on a forthcoming bond forfeited). 22 Sep 1845.

36. Goods and chattels of Benjamin S. MORRIS - $66.12 which John P. MORGAN recovered against said MORRIS as well for a certain debt as for interest thereon. 6 May 1844.

37. Goods and chattels of Lewis W. CABELL, Clifford CABELL and Richard H. GILLIAM - $2359.82 which the President, Directors & Company of the Farmers Banks of Virginia recovered against said CABELLs and GILLIAM on a delivery bond forfeited. 22 Apr 1844.

38. Goods and chattels of Edmund W. CABELL - $10 to satisfy Charles J. RYAN recovered against said Edmund W. CABELL. 7 Oct 1844.

39. Goods and chattels of Robert MOORE, administrator of Mary WRIGHT, dec'd - $12.41 which Edward M. W. DURPHEY recovered against him for costs expended in defending a certain action of ... by said Robt. MOORE against the said E. M. W. DURPHEY lately commenced(?). 12 June 1843.

40. Goods and chattels of Jonathan CHRISTIAN and Charles PATTISON - $410.20 which George H. MATTHEWS admr of Philip DUVAL, dec'd, who sues for the benefit of James C. WALTON, recovered against said CHRISTIAN & PATTISON (on a delivery bond forfeited). Apr 1844.

41. Goods and chattels of Thomas W. ISBELL & William ISBELL - $78.84 which William D. CHRISTIAN recovered against Thos. W. & William ISBELL (on a forthcoming bond forfeited). 12 Dec 1843.

42. Goods and chattels of William M. THURMOND - $563.66 which James T. SMITH and John W. MOSBY, who sue for the benefit of John

THOMPSON, Jr., and Joseph K. IRVING to the extent of one moiety of the debt recovered against him. 6 Jan 1843.

ADJUDGED DEBTS AND COURT CHARGES
CIRCA 1841

Below are extracts from adjudged debts and court charges. The receipts of monies collected have been omitted, also the sheriff's commission in each case and in most instances the interests have been omitted. The first party is the recipient of the award.

LINTHICUM & WINGFIELD vs Thos. WINGFIELD $18.82

BALDWIN vs MOORE & wife - $24.20

Wm. W. FERGUSON & Co. vs PHELPS' admr - $11.19

NUNNALLY vs Wm. H. MATTHEWS - $92.00. Levied on 2 horses. D. Bond taken & forfeited.

MOORE vs P. H. LOVERN[?] - $6.25 damage $5.00

YANCY vs WILLIAMS & MOSELEY - $50.00.

MILLER assn of WALTON vs J & P PAMPLIN $35.36.

Lined through is following:

~~FORBES (Extr) vs S. PANKEY~~

Wm. W. FERGUSON vs Chs. COLEMAN - Due 31st July 1840 $147.16. Levied on 4 horses. D. Bond taken & forfeited.

Wm. W. FERGUSON & Co. vs Joseph BURKS. Debt due 31st July 1840 $96.96.

BRANCH & COLEMAN vs Wm. A. KITCHEN. Debt due 1st Aug 1841 $38.13. Levied on 2 horses. D. Bond. Taken & forfeited.

T. GOOCH & CHEATWOOD vs Wm. A. KITCHEN. Debt due 1st Apl. 1839 - 137.99. Levied on 3 horses, 2 yoke of oxen, 3 milk cows & ten herd of sheep. D. Bond & forfeited.

FRANKLIN assn vs T. J. WALKER. Amt. execution due 10th Octo 1840 - $828.30.

Wm. FERGUSON & Co. vs. PHELPS' admr. Debt due 31st July 1838 - $426.11. By cash the proportion of the sale of a negro man Ned $434.00.

VAWTER vs J. A. CHICK. Debt due 1 Jany 1839 - $61.77. Levied on one horse & carryall. D. Bond taken & forfeited.

S P. VAWTER ...? vs Jas. A. CHICK & W. HIX. Debt due on D. Bd. 22nd May 1841 - 74.76.

John DAN & co. vs Henry A. CHRYTIAN[?]. Interest to 1st May 1841 - 46.30. Levied on one Negro woman NANCY. D. Bond taken & forfeited.

GOOCH & CHEATWOOD vs D. H. FERGUSON. Debt due 11 Jany 1841 - 186.54. Levied on one Negro woman MARY. D. Bond taken & forfeited.

FORD vs Tho. AUSTIN. Debt due Augst 1838 - $320.65. Levie on one Negro man FIELD. D. Bond taken & forfeited.

G. E. WILKINSON vs Th. AUSTIN, Exts. Debt 18th Jany. 1841 - $152.95. Levie on one Negro Man BILLY. D. Bond taken & forfeited.

FURGUSON & Co. vs Wilson HIX. Debt due 31st July 1837 - $349.51. Levie on one Negro boy NELSON. D. Bond taken & forfeited.

VAWTER vs FRANKLIN & BRYANT. Debt due 31st Feb 1839 - $54.25. Levie on one cow & calf, one feather bed, one pine press, two tables & 1/2 doz chairs.

Stephen W. CHRISTIAN vs Robt. P. PHELPS admr. Debt due 2nd Sept. 1837 - $372.32. Received June 20th 1841 349.68 it being proportion of $800 the sale of a Negro man NED in part of the ...? stated execution Chs. L. CHRISTIAN for Stephen W. CHRISTIAN.

R. [Robert] BRAZELEY vs R. P. PHELPS admr. Debt due 3rd Sept. 1836 - 27.13. Int. to 14th June 1841 - 7.78. Cost - 8.73. Returned no affects.

FLOOD & TRENT vs. Th. W. THORNHILL. Amt. debt due 1st Augs 1839 - 97.07. Int. to 3rd Mar 1841 - 9.27. Off then paid to pltff. 90. Int till 3rd Decr. 1841 - .73. Cost - 7.74.

BURTON & Co. vs Wm. H. MATTHEWS. Debt due 1st Apl. 1840 - 79.28. Off then paid R. SHAW - 22.00.

GLOVER's admrs vs MATTHEWS & SCRUGGS. Debt due 6th May 1840 -$60. Levied on 2 horses of E. L. Scruggs. D. Bond taken & forfeited.

RIVES & WHITE vs [Jas. T.] SMITH & Wm. M. THURMOND. Amt. debt due 15th July 1841 - 90.74. By 97 [bushels] wheat sold to Rives & White @ 92 cents - $87.39.

TINDALL assee[?] vs Jona. P. & Robt. PHELPS. To debt due on D.B. 29th Octo. 1840 - 132.25. Off former shffs tickets - 7.89.

Josiah MOSELY vs Wm. B. & Wm. W. MOSELEY. Debt due 1st January 1841 $85. Levie on one negro boy BEN. D. Bond taken & forfeited.

Geo. BOOKER exr of Sam JONES vs S. J. WALKER. Debt due 14th Jany 1839 - 2125.00. Levie on 3 Negro men, DAVY, CHARLES & JOHN. D. Bond taken & forfeited.

BOOKER's Exr vs Benja. PATTESON. Amt. debt due 26th Sept. 1832 - $53.75. Levied on gray horse & one gray mare. D. Bond taken & forfeited.

GOOCH & CHEATWOOD vs Henry LINTHICUM. Debt due 17th October 1839 - 135.18. Levied on 4 horses. D. Bond taken & forfeited.

Granville NUNNALLY vs MATTHEWS & CHRISTIAN. Debt on Dy., Bond 6th Apl. 1841 - 111.03.

SMITH &C. for G. M. PAYNE & W.C. MOSELEY vs Wm. M. THUR-MOND. Debt due 7th Jany. 1840 - 563.66. Levied on one Negro man EDMUND and one Negro woman FRANKEY forth coming bond taken & forfeited.

GOOCH & CHEATWOOD vs Daniel P. WATSON. Debt due 8th July 1840 - 75.94. Levied on 1 boy man & 5 head of cattle. D. Bond taken & forfeited.

LINTHICUM's Exr vs LINTHICUM & FLOOD. Amt Judgement for cost - 8.24.

J. T. BOCOCK Exr of Jno. FLOOD vs R. D. PALMER. Amt. Judgement for cost - 4.15.

Nathan SPENCER vs Dd. & Lot SPENCER. Debt due on D. Bond 7th Octr. 1840 - 230.60.

GOOCH & CHEATWOOD vs Wm. A. KITCHEN. Debt due 1st Apl. 1839 - 139.99. Levied on two horses, ten head of cattle & 8 head of sheep.

GOOCH & CHEATWOOD vs W. A. KITCHEN & A. D. ABRAHAM. Debt due on D. Bd. 1 June 1841 - 173.34.

S. P. VAWTER vs CARTER & ISBELL. Debt due 1st May 1838 - $100.00

BRANCH & HOLEMAN vs Wm. A. KITCHEN &c. [Wm. H. MAT-THEWS]. Debt due May 7, 1841 - $49.86. Int. till Octo. 11, 184 - 1.27. Cost - 5.08.

Genl. M. JOHNSON vs Wm. BURKS, T. P. WRIGHT & CARTER[?]. Debt due 1st Jany 1841 - 180. Then paid 115. Int. on $65 from 1st Jany 1841 to 11th Octo. 1841 - 3.04. Cost - 7.49.

GOOCH & CHEATWOOD vs Richd. PHELPS. Debt due 10th July 1839 - 56.18. Levied on one Negro woman EADY. D. Bond taken & forfeited.

Silas P. VAWTER vs CARTER & ISBELL. Debt due 1 May 1838 - 100.

Geo. S. DUGID & Co. vs Wm. Th. MATTHEWS. Debt due 8th Feby 1841 - 185. Levied on one Negro woman KATY. D. Bond taken & forfeited.

Saml. FORD S P vs Th. AUSTIN & R. H. GILLIAM. Debt due on D. B. 7th May 1841 - 281.93. [Execution] on the opposite page, Saml. FORD Sp &c. vs Thos. AUSTIN & R. H. GILLIAM has been settled by me & the plaintiffs ... Wm. M. MOSELY.

George E. WILKINSON vs Th. AUSTIN & R. H. GILLIAM. Debt due 7th May 1841 on D. Bd. - 170.82.

Geo. BOOKER Exr of Sam JONES vs Saml. J. WALKER & R. H. GIL-LIAM. Amt. Judgement on D. Bd. July 12th 1841 - $1451.83.

Mary GLOVER's admr vs Ed S. SCRUGGS & W. H. MATHEWS. Amt. Judgement on D. Bd. June 7th 1841 - 75.74.

Wm. W. FERGUSON &c vs Jane S. HANES. Debt due July 31st 1840 - 223.38. Levied on one Negro man FAYETTE. D. Bond taken & forfeited.

Wm. W. FERGUSON & Co. vs Andrew S. WHEELER Exr of Peter JOHNSON. Amt. debt due 31st July 1839 - 694.66. Levied on one Negro man TOM. Delivery Bond taken & forfeited.

Wm. W. FERGUSON &c. vs Chs. COLEMAN & A. CONNER. Debt due on D. Bd. 26th June 1841 - 170.

Wm. W. FERGUSON & Co. vs Saml. J. WALKER. Debt due 31st July 1840 - $489.59.

GOOCH & CHEATWOOD vs Wm. W. ALVIS. Debt due April to 1839 - $68.82.

Rob SHAW vs Wm. H. MATHEWS. Debt due 15th May 1838 - $79.76. Levied on one negro woman KATY. Delivery bond taken and forfeited.

Obadiah MOORE vs J. P. PHELPS admr of C. PHELPS. Debt due 23rd Feby. 1840 - $65. Damages - 22.08. Levied one Negro boy ISAAC. D. Bd. taken & forfeited.

J. W. FLOOD for Th. H. FLOOD vs Th. & Wm. ISBELL. Debt due on D. Bd. 4th May 1840 - 915.56.

R. P. COBBS for &c. vs. Wm. A. KITCHEN. Debt due 2nd Mch 1841 - $15.55. Levied on three horses. Delivery bond taken & forfeited.

Thos. P. WRIGHT vs Wm. A. KITCHEN & T. AUSTIN. Debt due 13th June 1841 - $41.40.

Reubin BROADAS vs Wm. & A. B. MEGGINSON. Debt due 24th Mch 1837 - $33.20. Levied on 2 horses. Delivery bond taken & forfeited.

Thos. W. THORNHILL vs Wilson HIX. Debt due 22nd Nov 1834 - $50. Levied on one negro man NELSON. Delivery bond taken.

CAMPBELL's Trustees vs WALKER & BRANCH. Debt due 1st May 1839 - $885. Levied on two negro men BEN & NATUS. D. Bond.

FORD vs Aren[?] KITCHEN & Clifd. CABELL. Amt. debt due 23rd Decr. - 1.20.

George W. KYLE vs William WALTON. Debt due 9th Octo. 1833 - 446.01. Off then paid order on J. P. PHILPS $105.

Geo. D. CORNISH vs Jno. W. WILLS. Amount debt due 24th Jany 1836 - 25.

Wm. W. FERGUSON &Co. vs Sally THORNHILL. Debt due July 31, 1840 - 96.64.

Thos. W. THORNHILL vs Wilson HIX. To debt due 27nd Nov 1834 - 50. Levied on one Negro man NELSON. D. Bond taken & forfeited.

S. FORD vs G. RUSH. Debt due 1st August 1833 - 30.23.

John H. JOHNSON vs Miland JOHNSON. To amt. debt due 11th Jany 1834 - 90.85.

Same vs same. To amt. debt on 12th Jany 1834 35.00.

Richard K. RAINE vs Danl. SWENEY. Debt due 3rd Sept. 1840 - 32.26.

Windslow ROBINSON & Thos. PUGH Trustees of James CAMPBELL vs S. J. WALKER & H. C. KYLE. Debt due on Dy Bond 27th Jany 1842 - 1066.41.

GOOCH & CHEATWOOD vs D. H. FERGUSON & C. J. JONES. Debt due 27th Decr. 1841 on D. Bd. - 214.47.

Robert SHAW vs Wm. H. MATHEWS & T. M. BONDURANT. Debt due on D. Bond 13th Decr. 1841 $107.75.

Robt. SHAW vs W. H. MATHEWS. Debt due on D. Bond 13th Decr. 1841 - 107.75.

Wm. W. FERGUSON vs Jane S., Jas. & Ro. HARRIS. Debt due on D. Bd. 3rd Nov 1841 - 259.64.

Saml. B. MEGGINSON vs. Jno. H. JOHNSON. Debt due 7th Sept. 1841 - 237.50.

Wm. W. FERGUSON &c. vs Saml. J. WALKER &c. To Amt. debt due on D. Bd. 4th Nov 1841 - 444.57.

Abram W. WIMBUSH vs BRANCH & S. J. WALKER. Amot. debt due June 27th 1841 - $2000. July 6th levied on 5 Negro men to wit BILLY, JOE, WILLIAM, PLEASANT & STEPHEN. D. Bond taken & forfeited.

Wm. W. FERGUSON &c. vs Mary S. PHELPS. Debt due 31st July 1840 - 225.85.

Lawrence ANDERSON vs Th. AUSTIN. Debt due 21st May 1840 - 59.14. Levied on 3 horses. D. Bond taken & forfeited.

Wilson HIX vs D. H. FERGUSON. Debt due 8th Nov 1840 - 50.41. Levied on 2 horses. D. Bond taken & forfeited.

Wm. D. CRISTIAN vs D. H. FERGUSON. Debt due 5th Octr. 1841 - 58.17. Levied on 3 horses. Delivery Bond taken & forfeited.

S. P. VAWTER vs D. H. FERGUSON. Debt due 24th Mar 1842 - 46.17. Levied on one Negro woman MARY. Delivery Bond taken & forfeited.

Wilson HIX vs Ro. B. PATTESON. Debt due 9th Feby 1841 - 58.91. Levied on 2 horses. Delivery Bond taken & forfeited.

FLOOD & NOWLIN vs Mary S. PHELPS. Debt due 31st Augst 1841 - 745.86. Levied on 4 Negro men, JOHN, NELSON, ALFRED & JACOB. D. Bond taken for ...

Th. WRIGHT vs Sam BRANCH & Ro. MOORE & B. G. BOOKER. Debt due 5th Sept. 1838 - 1081.82. Levied on 12 mules & one Jack the property of Ro. MOORE & two Negro men, JIM & BEN, the property of B. G. BOOKER. Delivery bond taken & forfeited.

Wm. H. WORD &c. vs Wm. H. MATHEWS. Debt due 31st Augs 1841 - 140.23. Levied on one Negro man JIM. Delivery bond taken & forfeited.

ELLIS Exr vs. Wm. H. MATHEWS. Debt due 1st Jany 1840 - 196.43. Levied on one Negro man, JIM. D.Bond taken & forfeited.

David ANDERSON Jr. &c. vs Wm. H. MATHEWS. Debt due 1st Apl. 1841 - 213.76. May 15 - Levied on one Negro man CULEY. Delivery bond taken & forfeited.

Willis CHAMBERS vs W. H. MATTHEWS. Debt due 25th Decr. 1840 - 100. Levied on one Negro woman Caley. Delivery bond taken & forfeited.

BRANCH & HOLEMAN for Wm. BRANCH vs Archibald AUSTIN. Debt due 1st Aug 1840 - 25.08. Levied on 1 horse. Delivery Bond taken & forfeited.

Wm. W. FERGUSON &C. vs Robert COLEMAN. Debt due 31st July 1840 - 146.23. Levied on 3 horses. Delivery Bond taken & forfeited.

Wm. W. FERGUSON &c. vs. J. P. PHELPS admr. Debt due 31st July 1839 - 158.74. Levied on one Negro boy ISAAC. Delivery bond taken & forfeited.

John W. CHAMBERS vs Wm.H. MATTHEWS. Debt due 1st Jany 1841 - 220. Levied on one Negro man JIM, 3 horses & Barouche. D. Bond taken & forfeited.

FLOOD & TRENT assee[?] &c. vs Philip WATKINS. Debt due 17th Jany 1840 - $352.71.

William W. FERGUSON &c. vs A. WHEELER exr of P. JOHNSON. Debt due 31st July 1840 - 51.58. Levied on 2 horses. D. Bond taken.

Saml. FORD vs John JOHNS. Debt due 15th May 1835 - 50. Levied on 2 horses. D. bond taken.

Geo. S. DUGID &C. vs Wm. H. MATHEWS. Debt due 8th Nov 1841 on D. bd. - 210.31.

Paul JONES vs S. D. PATTESON. Amt. debt due 25th Apl. 1842 -98. Satisfied by the sale of a coach & four horses, which sold for $255.

Hugh & Chs. RAINE vs. Bernard & Archer AUSTIN. Debt due 1st Octo. 1841 - 505.10.

Stephen CHRISTIAN vs Jonathan P. PHELPS ...? Amt. .... 10.53.

Wm. W. FERGUSON &co. vs Jonathan P. PHELPS. Amt. .. for cost - 11.79.

R. P. COBBS for GUY & BENTLY vs Wm. A. KICHIN & Th. AUSTIN. Debt due on D. Bd. 13th Decr. 1841 - 61.71.

James PANKEY Commissioner who sues for the benefit of Joel SIMMONS vs John PANKEY. Debt due 1st Apl 1841 - 525.

J. T. BOCOCK curator of the Est of Thos. WINFIELD vs Robert PHELPS. Debt due 31st Decr. 1827 - 277.28.

Elizabeth PHELPS vs Robert PHELPS. Debt due 1st June 1840 - 73.25.

Wm. D. JONES vs Jno. P. TALLEY. Debt due 1st Sept. 1840 - 426.26.

MOSELEY, SPENCER &Co. vs J. P. TALLY. Debt due 1st March 1842 - 194.78.

Th. H. FLOOD vs Th. W. ISBELL. Debt due 4th Sept. 1840 - 225. Levied on Negro man FREDERICK advertised to be sold at July court & proceedings stayed by an injunction.

FLOOD & TRENT vs Th. W. ISBELL. Debt due 1st Augs 1840 - 273.86. Levied on one Negro man PETER. Proceedings stopped by an injunction.

Laurence ANDERSON vs Th. W. ISBELL. Debt due 13th May 1841 - 172.97. May 31, 1842 - Levied on one Negro man PETER & proceedings stayed by an injunction.

James ANDERSON vs Th. W. ISBELL. Debt due 19th Octr. 1840 - 146.22. May 31, 1842 - Levied on one Negro boy JOE & proceedings stopped by an injunction.

Wm. D. CHRISTIAN vs Th. W. ISBELL. Debt due 24th Decr. 1840 - 75.22. May 31, 1842 - Levied on one Negro boy JOE & proceedings stayed by an injunction.

FLOOD & NOWLIN vs Th. W. ISBELL. Debt due 31st August 1840 - 173.74. Levied on 1 Negro boy ISHAM & proceedings stayed by an injunction.

Th. TRENT vs Th. W. ISBELL. Debt due 1st Aus 1841 - 26.87. May 31 - Levied on one Negro boy ISHAM & proceedings stopped by an injunction

Wm. W. FERGUSON & Co. vs James PAMPLIN. Amt. debt due 31 July 1840 - 79.50. Nov 23 - Cr By the sale of the following property - By 19 3/5 bbls com 255 pr bl $49.98. By 1 1/2 bbls short corn 1.10 - 1.65. 3 stacks blade fodder 15 pr - 7.50. To Top stack & Shucks[?] - 10.

Th. W. THORNHILL vs W. HIX & Co. Debt due 25th Decr 1841 - 84.70.

R. BROADUS for &c. vs A. B. MEGGINSON &co. Debt due 3rd Nov 1841 - 79.99.

Wm. W. FERGUSON vs Jas. M. HARRIS. Debt due 31st July 1837 -109.47.

Wm. P. OLIVER [assignee] vs Wm. H. MATHEWS. Debt due 10th May 1841 - 28. Levied 13th June 1842 on one horse. Delivery Bond taken & forfeited.

Asa STRATTON &C. vs W. H. MATHEWS. Debt due 10th May 1841 - 54.92. Levied 10th June 1842 on a barouche. D. Bond taken & forfeited.

R. P. COBB for D. ANDERSON Jr. & Co. [vs] Th. AUSTIN. Debt due 2nd Octo. 1841 - 24.91. Levied on 1 horse. D. Bond taken & forfeited.

R. P. COBBS for D. BULLINGTON &c. vs A. AUSTIN. Debt due 3rd Jany 1842 - 63.16. Levied on 2 mules. D.Bd. taken & forfeited.

Jno. SHACKLEFORD vs S. F. SPELLER. Debt due 17th Decr 1841 -77.98. Levied on 3 horses. D.Bond taken & forfeited.

Frederick W. SHRAP[?] sp[?] vs W. H. MATHEWS. Debt due 10th Nov 1840 - 60.71. Levied on one Negro woman Katey. D. Bond taken & forfeited.

Josiah HATCHER vs Wm. B. SHEPPARD. Debt due 1st Mar 1841 - 35.73. Int. till 18th June - 1842 - 2.72. Cost - 6.77.

S. H. PAROCK vs SHEPPARD. Debt due 31st Octo. 1840 - 36. Int. till 13th June 1842 - 3.5. cost - 6.12.

C. D. COLEMAN & Jno. C. TRENT, trustees for Henry B. BRANCH vs Wm. B. SHEPPARD. Debt due 1st Mar 1841 - 81.15.

J. WATTS admr vs Jas C. FON. Debt due 20th Octo. 1841 - 28.

Jas. WATTS admr vs Jas C. FON & J. MOSELEY. Debt due June 20th 1841 - 30.95.

Jonas M. TAPSCOTT vs Bernard & Archer AUSTIN. Debt due on Dy Bd. 9th Decr 1841 - 65.35.

James BLANTON vs GREGORY & FORE. Amo. due April 21, 1841 - $175. May 21, 1842 - Levie on 1 Negro woman CREATED[?].

FLOOD & TRENT for P. A. WATKINS vs Philip WATKINS. Debt due 17th Jany 1840 - 352.71. Levied on one Negro boy JIM. Delivery Bond taken & forfeited.

Wm. W. FERGUSON & Co. vs Wilson HIX & R. H. GILLIAM. Debt due 1st June 1841 - 457.26.

Th. WORD [assignee] of Jas H. DAVIS vs Bernard & Archibald AUSTIN. Debt due Octo 16th 1841 - 112.51.

Reuben P. COBBS for D. BULLINGTON &c. vs. Archer & B. AUSTIN. Debt due on D. Bd. 3rd June 1842 - 75.02.

Samuel FORD ...? vs Archer BERNARD & Th. AUSTIN. Debt due 10th May 1841 - 521.24.

By the sale of a negro woman SALLY & 2 children sold to A. D. ABRAHAM. Satisfied & paid to Chs L. CHRISTIAN agst for S. FORD. Cr by $72.30 paid Sep 12th 1842.

Patrick H. JACKSON Trustee for A. VENABLE. Debt due 23rd June 1841 - 33.77.

Edward B. MILLER vs Jno. MORRIS & N. H. THORNTON. Debt due 20th May 1842 - 117.36.

John T. BOCOCK vs William MEGGINSON. Debt due for Execution - 552.05. Off then paid by sale of stock crop of oats & fodder, household & kitchen furniture, plantation tools &c. - $183.52.

Wm. MILLER exr of Jno. PITTMAN vs Th. W. ISBELL. Amount due Decr. 22, 1831 - 45. Levied June 22nd 1842 on 2 horses. D. Bond taken & forfeited.

Chs. McKINEY, assa[?] vs Geo. E. WATSON. Amount due Jany 1st 1842 - 135.50. Int. till Oct 10th 1842 - 6.31. Cost - 6.37.

Jno. C. SHACKLEFORD vs S. F. SPELLER &c. Debt due 24th May 1842 - 91.02.

Geo. M. PAYNE & Wm. C. MOSELEY vs Wm. M. THURMOND & Wm. THORNHILL....

Levi WEBB vs J. P. MORGAN &Co. Debt due 1st June 1842 - 63.23.

Wm. LEITCH vs John GARROTT & Co. Amo. due 10th June 1842 - 314.93. Aug 23, 1842 - By cash paid J. HILL - $150. Sept 12 by Cash pd J. Hill - 100.

Laurence ANDERSON vs Th. AUSTIN & A. AUSTIN. Debt due 2nd May 1842 - 74.97.

P. H. HICKOK [assignee] vs Th. W. AGEE & W. A. COBBS. Debt due 8th Apl. 1841 - 58.50.

Moseley SPENCER &c. vs Charlotte FORBES &c. Debt due 1st June 1842 - 93.77.

Moseley SPENCER &c. vs Jno. MORRIS SH &co. amt. due 1st June 1842 - 83.15.

John M. WRIGHT exr of Th. WRIGHT, decd. vs Ro. MOORE, B. G. BOOKER & A. R. JONES. Debt due 1st June 1842 - $1365.91.

FLOOD & TRENT [assignee] vs Philip WATKINS &c. Debt due 1st June 1842 - 247.30.

Obadiah MOORE vs Mary PHELPS. Debt due 1st Jany 1842 - 108.57.

MOSELEY's trustee vs Wm. H. MATHEWS. Amount due 12th Apl. 1842 - 223.30.

J. SPELLER, gdn [guardian] vs Wm. A. GILLISPIE & J. GLOVER. Debt due 25th Decr. 1841 - 91. Off paid G. A. SPELLER - 27.46.

Jno. W. CHAMBERS vs Wm. H. MATHEWS. Debt due 1st June 1842 - 257.74.

Fred W. KNAP sp vs Wm. H. MATHEWS. Debt due June 10th 1842 - 77.03.

Moseley SPENCER &c. vs Jno. P. MORGAN. Debt due 1st June 1842 - 263.34. By the sale of FILLIS - $175. By cash G. D. SAUNDERS - 100. By the bal of McKENNY's Draft - 16.46.

Wm. P. OLIVER vs W. H. MATHEWS & S. P. HARDWICK. Debt due 13th June 1842 - 37.74.

Thos. PAROCK sp vs W. H. MATHEWS. Debt due 10th June 1842 - 69.31.

R. P. COBBS for Dd ANDERSON Jr. &Co. vs Th. AUSTIN 8c. Debt due 2nd July 1842 - 34.57.

Samuel FORD vs Jno. JOHNS &c. Debt due July 1st 1842 - 78.83.

Wm. PATTESON admr of Ro. P. PHELPS vs Charles THOMAS. Amt. Judgment for cost - 4.26.

Wm. W. FERGUSON &c. vs Sally THORNHILL. Debt due July 31st 1840 -96.64.

Wm. W. FERGUSON &c. vs Jno. P. PHELPS admr of Charles PHELPS decd. Debt due 6th May 1842 - 193.50.

Wm. W. FERGUSON &Co. vs Ro. COLEMAN. Debt due 18th May 1842 -80.12.

Th. TRENT vs Thos. W. ISBELL. Debt due 1st Augst 1841 - 26.87. Levied on one Negro man FREDRICK. Delivery Bond taken & forfeited.

H. PERKINS vs Jno. W. WILLS. Amt. cash due 1st Mar 1837 - 14.26.

Wm. A. MILLER exr of John PITTMAN vs Th. W. & Wm. ISBELL. Debt due 22nd June 1842 - 84.73.

Wilson HIX vs D. H. FERGUSON &c. Debt due 1st June 1842 - 65.90.

Wm. D. CHRISTIAN vs D. H. FERGUSON &c. Debt due 21st May 1842 - 71.64.

Wm. W. FERGUSON & Co. vs Samuel F. SPELLER. Debt due 31st January 1842 - 217.25.

William BRANCH vs J. M. & Th. AUSTIN. Debt due 30th Apl. 1842 - 1054.

The President Directors & Co. of the Bank of Va. vs. Jno. J[ames] MORRIS & Jno. MORRIS, N[athan] H. THORNTON. Debt due 6th Octo. 1841 - 902.68.

FLOOD & NOWLIN vs Mary S. PHELPS & W. D. CHRISTIAN. Debt due 6th May 1842 - 808.09.

BRANCH & HOLEMAN for Wm. BRANCH vs Archd. AUSTIN & Th. AUSTIN. Debt due 1st June 1842 - 36.73.

Thos. TRENT vs Th. W. ISBELL. Debt due 1st Oct 1842 - $38.04.

GOOCH & CHEATWOOD for GOOCH vs Wm. D. CHRISTIAN admr of G. CHRISTIAN. Debt due 1st Apl. 1840 - 73.32.

Wm. W. FERGUSON vs Jno. PHELPS. Received June 1st 1843, $30 + plus commission.

S. P. VAWTER vs D. H. FERGUSON &Co. Debt due 24th May 1842 - 58.91.

[pages missing]

Octo. 4th 1842 - Levied on one Negro men FREDRICK. Delivery Bond taken & forfeited. [previous page missing which would indicate for whom the judgement was awarded.]

Received Decr 8th 1843 Th. H. FLOOD in case vs Th. W. ISBELL & Wm. ISBELL.

FLOOD & NOWLIN vs Thos. W. ISBELL. Debt due 31st Augs 1840 - 173.74. Levied on one Negro man JOE. Delivery bond taken & forfeited.

James ANDERSON vs Thomas W. ISBELL. Debt due 9th Octo. 1840 - 156.22. Int. till 1st Octo. 1842 - 18.50. Cost - 8.16. Octo. 1st 1842 - Levied on one Negro man ALLEN. Delivery bond taken & forfeited.

William D. CHRISTIAN vs Th. W. ISBELL. Debt due 24th Decr. 1840 - 75.22. Levied on one Negro man ALLEN. Delivery Bond taken & forfeited.

Laurence ANDERSON vs Thomas W. ISBELL. Debt due 13th May 1841 - 172.97. Octo. 3rd 1842 - Levied on one Negro man FREDRICK. Bond taken & forfeited.

FLOOD & TRENT for Thos. TRENT vs Thomas W. ISBELL. Debt due 1st Augs 1840 - $273.86. Octo. 1st 1842 - Levied on one Negro PETER. Delivery bond taken & forfeited.

Charles McKINNEY vs Jno. P. MORGAN. Debt due 30th May 1842 - 58.20. Octo. 20, 1842 - Levied on one Negro boy, JIM. Delivery bond taken & forfeited.

Thomas FORBES vs Jno. P. MORGAN. Debt due 2nd March 1838 - 117.51. Octo. 22, 1842 - Levied on one Negro boy JIM. Delivery bond taken & forfeited.

William W. FERGUSON &Co. vs James PHELPS W. J. Debt due 8th Mar 1841 - 111.49. Int. till 28th Sept. 1842 - 10.40. Cost - 8.70.

Fredrick G. PETERS s.p. vs Edmd. W. CABELL. Debt due 1st May 1832 - 102.19. July 30th 1842 - Levied on one Negro boy JOE. Delivery Bond taken & forfeited.

Buckingham Justices for Chs. McKINNEY exr of P. FRANCISCO vs Jno. MORRIS & Silas WATKINS. Debt due 7th Apl. 1838 - 705.38. Levied on two Negro men HAN & FRANK. Delivery Bond taken & forfeited.

FLOOD & TRENT vs Samuel J. WALKER. Debt due 15th Feby 1842 - 212. Octo 15th 1842 - Levied on one Negro boy WILLIAM. Delivery Bond taken & forfeited.

Thomas TRENT vs Saml. J. WALKER. Debt due 1st Augs 1841 - 116.58. Octo. 15th 1842 - Levied on one Negro man BEN. Delivery bond taken & forfeited.

William PATTESON vs John WEBB. Debt due 1st Octo. 1827 - 348.32. Nov 1st 1842 - Levied on two Negro woman EASTER & NICY. Delivery bond taken & forfeited.

J. & E. B. MOSELEY vs S. P. HARDWICK. Debt due 1st Jany 1842 - 109.14. Nov 1st 1842 - Levied on four horses. delivery bond taken & forfeited.

Jackquelin TAYLOR vs Wilson HIX & Wm. THORNHILL. Debt due 7th Sept. 1841 - 1891.81. Levied on one Negro man NELSON, one woman MARIA & 2 children, one woman SELVY & child, six horses, one waggon & harness & one stud. Delivery bond taken & forfeited.

Jackquelin TAYLOR vs Wilson HIX. Debt due 29th Octo. 1840 -1040.65. Augs 29, 1842 - Levied on Five Negroes, MARIA & 2 children, SELVY & one child. Delivery bond taken & forfeited.

Nelson THORNHILL admr vs Sally THORNHILL. Debt due 10th May 1842 - 80.87. Octo. 10 - Levied on one horse & Negro girl NANCY. Delivery bond taken & forfeited.

Moseley SPENCER &c. vs David W. GLOVER. Debt due 1st Jany 1842 - 55.35. Octo. 20, 1842 - Levied on 3 horses. delivery bond taken & forfeited.

Thomas TRENT vs Wm. D. CHRISTIAN. Debt due 2nd Nov 1841 - 357.88. Decr. 3rd 1843 - Levied on 5 horses. Delivery bond taken & forfeited.

Moseley SPENCER &c. vs James C. FON for est S. FON. Debt due 1st March 1841 - 176.10. Levied on one Negro woman NICY. Delivery bond taken & forfeited.

Thos. JOHNS vs James JONES. Debt due 29th Nov 1840 - 400. Levied on 2 Negro men CHARLES & JOHN. Delivery bond taken & forfeited.

Isaac R. REYNOLDS vs John S. GLOVER & Jno. GLOVER. Debt due 9th May 1842 - 431. Nov 20th 1842 - Levied on four horses & ten head of cattle. Delivery bond taken & forfeited.

Silas P. VAWTER vs Jno. WADE. Debt due 8th Mar 1842 - 80. Levied on 4 horses. Delivery bond taken & forfeited.

Silas P. VAWTER vs Joel WATKINS. Debt due 7th Octo. 1841 - 211. Levied on one Negro man STEPHEN. Delivery bond taken & forfeited.

Thomas TRENT vs Wyatt ABBOTT. Debt due 18th Augs 1841 - 65.49. Levied on one bay mare, one yoke of oxen, one ox cart, two cows & calves. Delivery bond taken & forfeited.

Dunlop MONCUN & Co. [assignee?] vs Wilson HIX. Debt due 3rd May 1841 - 376.92. Levied on two Negro men, JORDIN & CHARLES. Delivery bond taken & forfeited.

J. T. SMITH for Wadworth JAMES &c. vs Wm. M. THURMOND. Debt due 25 Decr. 1840 - $563.66. March 2nd - Levied on one Negro man WILSON. Delivery bond taken & the property delivered on the day of sale & the sale stopped by an injunction.

Moseley SPENCER &Co. vs J. P. MORGAN & Wm. W. FORBES. To this amt. being the bal. of execution paid by J. J. WALKER & for his benefit 12th Decr. 1843 - 100.

HOCKER & NICHOLAS vs. Th. W. AGEE. Debt due 1st March 1841 - 32.02.

A & W. H. PLUNKET for W. H. PLUNKET vs Jos. S. DILLARD. Debt due 1st June 1842 - 57.50.

Saml. FORD vs Creed KITCHEN & C. CABELL. Debt due 23rd Apl. 1840 - 30.

Hugh RAINE [assignee?] of H. D. FLOOD vs Abednego CONNER. Debt due 1st July 1842 - 23.50.

H. RAINE assee vs Stephen PANKEY. Debt due 1st July 1842 - 20.94.

FLOOD & TRENT for Th. TRENT vs Th. W. & W. ISBELL. Debt due 1st Octo. 1843 - 262.22.

CHEATWOOD for MOSELEY vs Th. WRIGHT & J. PHELPS. Debt due 9th Feby 1842 - 128.

PROMISSORY NOTES AND RECEIPTS

Many of the transactions relate the hiring out of a slave. In each instance the agreement required returning the slave with a certain quantity and quality of clothes, "furnished with a hat and blanket."

1. Received of Mr. Chas. CONNER a negro girl (PHILLIS) conveyed to us (as trustees) by said CONNER & Charles L. MAXEY for the benefit of Martha & Ouesby MAXEY - March 25, 1828. William SPENCER, John MORGAN. Witness: Lott SPENCER.

2. ... I promise to pay to Little Berry HARDIMON or his assigns ... $300 Current Money of Virginia in the purchase of a negro woman LUCY. 7 Dec 1829. Charles HARDIMAN. Test. John MORRIS.

3. Mr. James BROWN. In use with Jno. AUSTIN, Dr. ... extracting 2 teeth Negro (SAM) pr $2.00. Receivd. payment. J. M. AUSTIN. 30th Dec: 1835.

4. Mr. Martin HURT. 1839. To R. H. GILLIAM, Admr. of S. GREGORY Dr. To Hire of Negro MARTHA, $20 - price I hired MARTHA to Martin HURT for the year 1839. Barnett HURT.

5. For $30 paid by William A. WINGFIELD of the county of Buckingham I have sold the right of my wife Sophia Jane formerly Sophia Jane REYNOLDS in two Negro slaves to wit, ELIZA and ELICK with the future increase of the females thereof being the slaves given to my said wife's mother Frances REYNOLDS and to her children by the last will and testament of her father, John PETTESON, decd. 4 March 1840. Thomas WINGFIELD. Witness. W. P. BOCOCK.

6. Mr. Richard H. GILLIAM - Sir you will please to send me the money that MARTHA sold for. After taking off $35 which you sent me by Jas. W. STUART & your commissions. Send the above by Mr. Saml. WRIGHT. Yours Respectfully. Barnet HURT. Oct. 10th 1840.

7. Memorandum - Having been this day present with R. H. GILLIAM & Barnet HURT with a settlement made this 27 Oct have arranged & looked over, settled all of these a/c exhibited before me & think their family stated both parties express their [they're] satisfied & the said GILLIAM has paid over to WRIGHT 747.79/100 in leash L89.46 to Mr. KING & WALKER & 37.75 to B. HURT hiself & Commission of sales of negro 40.00. Oct 27-1840. Josiah MOSELEY.

8. Mr. Barnett Hurt. 1840. Bought of SNILLING & PENY. Dec, 31. 5 hogs 1145w @ 6.50. 74.42.

"Majr. R. H. GILLIAM. Sir. You'l. please pay $74.42 and hire out RANDOLPH & MILEY for the best price you can, and hold the bonds until you are paid, Barnett HURT. Dec 1840."

9. 25.00. On or before 1 Jan next, we, Madison H. BAYLEY and Joseph T. LIGON promise to pay to Richard H. GILIAM $25 for the hire of a Negro Slave named ELICK for the present year. Said slave to be returned at Christmas next, well clothed with customary Clothing, and fur-

nished with a Hat and Blanket. 18 Jan 1844. M. H. BAYLEY. Jos. T. LIGON.

10. On or before 1 Jan next I promise to pay Richard H. GILLIAM trustee for Frs. REYNOLDS $27.50 for hire of negro boy ELICK; said negro to be returned on 25th Dec next. 23 Jan 1845. Jos. T. LIGON

11. The Sheriff is authorized to hire out a negro man DANEL to the · highest bidder or privately for the shortest time that will pay the tax & arrears of tax due by me.... 27 Nov 1844. E. W. CABELL.

12. Mr. Berry HARDIMAN. 1844. In a/c with J. J. WALKER & Co. Nov. 19th - 1 pair Bed Blankets 5.00. Dec 20 - 1 White wool hat 1.00. Due 1 July 1845 - $6.00

13. Recd. of Jno. MORGAN by the honor of R. H. GILLIAM $16.26 cents being his part for the price of CAMBELL, a negro which he bought. 13 Jan 1845. H. A. WALDEN.

14. Received Jan 9 1845 of Richard H. GILLIAM. $16.66 due from his lot of negroes drawn in the Est[ate] of Richard GILLIAM being No. 3 to No. 4 which was drawn by me, Sally W. NEIGHBOURS. Test. W. NEIGHBOURS.

15. On or before 25 Dec next I promise to pay Richard H. GILLIAM $75 for the hire of a negro man JACK for the present year. 22 Jan 1842. /s/Art. W. GILLIAM.

16. [Consent of executors of the estate of Archibald AUSTIN to allow sheriff's sale of slaves, DICK, AARON, PAGE, SUKEY in payment of debts owed by Archibald AUSTIN, one of the heirs]. Negro men, DICK & AARON, to be sold on the second Monday in August next, .. and said Archibald AUSTIN being further bound on other exions [actions] which are to be satisfied on the 2nd Monday in the present month, the said Sheriff may at that time sell One negro man PAGE & one Negro girl SUKEY. 5 July, 1842. J. M. AUSTIN, Th. AUSTIN, extrs. of Archd. AUSTIN, decd.

17. 1842. Thos. W. ISBELL.

To shff. of Buckingham

Amt Jas. ANDERSON's Execution	218.28		
" S. ANDERSONS Dr	231.34		
FLOOD & NOWLIN Dr.	244.80		
Th. H. FLOOD	284.56		
Flood & HUNT	296.70		
W. P. BOCOCK	307.56		
	1579.24		
By R. H. GILLIAM ...?	296.92		
" Sale of ALLEN	225		
" " of JOE	450		
PETER	500		
Off NOTE[?]	13.98	486.02	1457.94
			121.30

18. On or before 25 Dec 1843 I promise to pay to Litelberry HAR-DIMAN $50 for the hire of Negro man TOM. 16 Jan 1843. Doctor S. WOOLDRIDGE. [His mark]

19. Th W. ISBELL. To R. H., GILLIAM Dr.
Cash paid bal. of Exn. to Wm. MILLER $37.46
Cash paid Th TRENTs[?] Executor[Execution?] 46.36
Cash lent   10
Amt. Tax   9.26   19.26

By this amount it being the purchase of two negro boys ISHAM & HENRY bought this day. 600.00
                   396.92

396.92 On or before 1 April next I promise to Thomas W. ISBELL $396.92. 11 March 1843. /s/ R. H. GILLIAM.

20. Executions Th W ISBELL

Jas. ANDERSON	218.28
L. ANDERSON	231.34
FLOOD & NOWLIN	240.80
Th H FLOOD	284.56

FLOOD & TRENT   296.74
Willis P BOCCOCK

                                 1271.72

By R H GILLIAM note		296.92	
Sale of ALLEN		225--	
Sale of JOE		450--	
Sale of PETER		500--	
Off note to T H PITTMAN	13.98	486.02	1457.94
			$186.22

1843 Augst 14th Cash paid to W P BOCOCK's exr. 186.22

21. Lewis W. CABELL and [blank] are bound unto Frederick G. PETERS surviving partner of himself and Willis H WILLIS decd. late merchants and partners trading under the firm & style of PETERS and WILLIS in the sum of $226.08 to be paid unto the said Frederick G. PETERS surviving partner &c. 15 Dec 1843.

Frederick G Peters surviving partner has sued out of the Circuit Superior Court of Law and Chancery for Buckingham Co., a writ of Fieri Facias against the goods and chattels of Lewis W. Cabell and obtained a judgement which amounts to $138.04: And Richard H Gilliam hath taken negro woman FANNY, property of Lewis W. CABELL.

22. .....? Lott SPENCER &c. Debt due on Dy. Bond- 13th May 1845
113.24

Int to 18th Sept. 1845	2.36
1/2 commiss not added	2.74
2 notices 1.00	119.34
	439.10

To amt your tax 17.02
Cash paid Jas. Brown on a/c of your note to SR
        Invoice   61.88
By 1 Negro boy GEORGE bought $510.00

23. Buckingham County Court June 1845. On the motion of Francis SAUNDERS he is exempt from the payment of taxes and levies on two negro slaves viz. NED & USLEY on account of age and infirmity.

24. Amt paid BOCOCK's debt $262.99
   Amt to be paid to BONDURANT's debt which is on Dy. Bond
   Amt to HARDIMAN's debt which is in Dy Bond
   The balance of five hundred & ten dollars to price of George, after deducting the debts above named I will pay to Mr. Spencer or towards a debt which he owes to the Revd. Saml. R. IRVING [Methodist] in or before the 1st Jany next this 10th July 1845.

25. $425. On demand I promise to pay Wm. M. MOSELEY $425 for his interest in negro slaves: AMANDA, MILLY & GEORGE. 19 Nov 1845. R. H. GILLIAM.

26. On or before 25 Dec 1845 we promise to pay unto Daniel P. WATSON $22.50 for the hre [hire] of a negro woman. 8 Jan 1845. /s/John R. WADE. /s/R. H. GILLIAM.

27. 12 months after date I promise to pay to Littleberry HARDIMAN $60 for the hire of his man TOM for the present year. 1 Jan 1846. Dr. Sawney WOODRIDGE [his mark]. Witness /s/ J. W. MEREDITH.

28. $300.00 We William McFADDEN, Charles HARDIMAN and Sally McFADDEN are bound unto John MORRIS, high Sheriff of Buckingham County $300. 6 May 1846. John H. JOHNSON has issued out a fieri facias against the goods and chattles of Francis McFADDIN and caused the same to be levied in a negro boy DAVY, and whereas Sally McFADDIN having obtained an injunction stopping the sale of the said negro boy Davy upon the conditions that the Sheriff of Buckingham hold the said negro boy in his possession or hire him out, so that he be forth coming at any time. /s/ William McFADDEN. /s/Charles HARDIMAN. /s/ Sally McFADDEN [her mark].

29. On or before 1 Jan next I will pay Nancy TALBOT $10 for the hire of Negro boy ROLERSON for the present year. 1 Jan 1847. /s/ Lewis T. MILLER.

30. On or before 25 Dec next we promise to pay Richard H. GILLIAM admr. of S. B. HARDIMAN decd. $25 for the hire of a negro boy RANDOLPH for the present year. 19 Feb 1847 /s/James H. FARLEY. /s/ Marshall P. THURMAN.

31. We John E. HARDIMAN in his own right and as attorney in fact for the children of Thomas HARDIMAN and Lawson G. TYLER are held bound unto Richard H. GILLIAM admr. of Littleberry HARDIMAN, decd. for $500. 16 Dec 1847.

By a decree of the County court of Buckingham pronounced on 13 Dec 1847 in a suit between Lawson G. TYLER and Elizabeth his wife plaintiffs, and Richard H. GILLIAM admr. of Littleberry HARDIMAN, decd and other defendants it was ordered that John MORRIS, John J. GILLIAM, Tandy HOLEMAN and Moses A. SPENCER, or any three of them, should divide the slaves of Littleberry HARDIMAN, decd, and allot to Anderson HARDIMAN, John E. HARDIMAN, Wm. HARDIMAN, Thomas HARDIMAN, Samuel HARDIMAN, Samuel SMITH and Judith his wife, John CROWES[?] and his wife Anna, Hardin GRIGGS and his wife Mary GRIGGS, Erastus M. DAVIDSON and his wife Lasamy[?], Susan HARDIMAN and Elizabeth HARDIMAN, one ninth part thereof on their or some one for them entering into a refunding bond with Security to the said Richard H. GILLIAM, admr., in the sum $500 and the said Richard H. GILLIAM, admr, as aforesaid having delivered over to the said John E. HARDIMAN, one ninth part of the said slaves belonging to the heirs of Thomas HARDIMAN, decd. Now if the said John E. HARDIMAN shall refund his due proportion (being one ninth) of any debts or demands which may hereafter appear against the estate of the said Littleberry HARDIMAN and the cost attending the collection of such debts then this obligation to be void else to remain in full force. Witness /s/ John E. HARDIMAN, John E. HARDIMAN, Attorney in fact for heirs. /s/William J. HARDIMAN. /s/Thomas HARDIMAN. /s/Lawson TYLER.

32. We, Anna MATTOX and Lawson G. TYLER are held bound to Richard H. GILLIAM, admr. of Littleberry HARDIMAN, decd. the sum of $500. 16 Dec 1847. Whereas by a decree of the county court of Buckingham pronounced on 13 Dec 1847 in a suit depending between Lawson G. TYLER and Elizabeth his wife, plaintiffs, and Richard H. GILLIAM admr. of Littleberry HARDIMAN, decd. and other defendants it was ordered and decreed that John MORRIS, Grandison MOSELEY, John J. GILLIAM, Tandy HOLMAN and Moses A. SPENCER or any three of them should divide the slaves of Littleberry HARDIMAN decd. and allot

to Anna MADDOX one ninth part thereof or her or some one for her entering into a refunding bond with security to Richard H GILLIAM admr as aforesaid in the sum of $500 and the said Richd. H. GILLIAM admr. having delivered over to the said Anna MADDOX one ninth part of the said slaves, if the said Anna MADDOX shall refund her due proportion of any debts or demands which shall in any way appear against the estate of the said Littleberry HARDIMAN and the cost attending the collection of such debts then this obligation to be void, else to remain in full force. Signed sealed & delivered in the present of Charles G. HAR-DIMAN by Samuel G. HARDIMAN. /s/Josiah MADDOX. /s/ Anna MADDOX. /s/Josiah MADDOX. /s/ Lawson TYLER.

33. We, Charles HARDIMAN and Anderson D. ABRAHAM are held and firmly bound into Richard H. GILLIAM, admr. of Littleberry HAR-DIMAN decd. in the sum $160. 14 Dec 1847. Whereas Chs. HAR-DIMAN became the purchaser of a certain old negro woman SUCKEY belonging to the estate of said L. B. HARDIMAN, by receiving the sum of $96 to support clothes and taken care of said negro SUCKEY during her natural life, now if the said Chs. HARDIMAN shall support clothes and take care of said old negro woman SUCKEY during her natural life so that she shall not be chargeable to the said est of L. B. HARDIMAN or the county of Buckingham, then this obligation to be void, else to remain in full force. /s/ Charles HARDIMAN. /s/ A. D. ABRAHAM.

Addition note: Received Dec 17 1847 of R. H. GILLIAM, admr. of Lit-tleberry HARDIMAN, decd, $96 in full for support of an old negro woman SUCKEY during her natural life. /s/Charles S. HARDIMAN.

34. Received April 10, 1848 of Richard H GILLIAM, admr. of Littleber-ry HARDIMAN, decd., the following negroes allotted as in a division made of the negroes belonging to the estate of Littleberry HARDIMAN decd., RANDOLPH a boy valued at five hundred dollars, PHEBE a woman valued at three hundred dollars and ROBERT a boy valued at two hundred & twenty five dollars and thirty two dollars & thirty three cents in money making in the whole one thousand fifty seven dollars & 33 cents, it being in full of our legacy as per report of commissioners. Signed by Charles S. HARDIMAN, Brightbury G. BABER, Samuel HAR-DIMAN, Samuel HARDIMAN guardian ... George H. HARDIMAN,

John HARDIMAN, William HARDIMAN, By Samuel HARDIMAN attorney.

35. Received of R H GILLIAM admr of Littleberry HARDIMAN, decd., two negroes TOM and SUCKEY and also fifteen dollars in money being the hire of TOM which is in full of my interest in the estate of Littleberry HARDIMAN decd. this the 15 Apl 1848. signed by Samuel HARDIMAN, attorney for George W. HARDIMAN. Teste: Charles G. HARDIMAN.

36. Memorandum of contract made 18 Jan 1849 between Edward J. GILLIAM of the first part and Spotswood JONES of the other part. Said E. J. GILLIAM has this day sold to the said S. JONES one negro woman EASTHER for and in consideration of the said Spotswood JONES agreeing to take & support during life two old negroes NELSON & his wife ANICA[?], and the said GILLIAM on his part guarantees to the said JONES & his heirs a good right and title to the said woman EASTHER & the said JONES binds himself to support the above old negroes. 1 Jan 1849. Signed E. J. GILLIAM, Spotswood JONES.

37. On or before 1 Jan 1851 I promise to pay to Geo H. MATHEWS $105 for the hire of a negro man ARCHER for the next year. 28 Dec 1849.

38. On or before 1 Jan 1852 I promise to pay, George H. MATHEWS $110 for the hire of a negro man ARCHE[?]. 14 Jan 1851.

39. Scottsville 13 Feb 1851. Col. GILLIAM. Dear Sir. ... If Col. BONDURANT was apprised of the term upon which he purchased the negro & I can scarcely support that he would buy without knowing.... . Of course we cannot force the Col to execute the note unless he is willing to do so ... - my love to Mrs. G. & cousin Virginia. ... Your Obedt. W. BRANCH.

40. I Henry C. THACKSTON of Prince Edward County, Virginia, having been appointed Guardian for Richard H., Harriet E. & Ann E. GILLIAM, children of John C. GILLIAM, decd, by the county court of Buckingham and have this day attended the settlement of Richard H. GILLIAM's account as their former Gdn and received an order on Wm. L. LANCASTER trustee for all the Estate of said children in his hands as reported by commissioner Bocock, and also bind myself ... to take charge

of a certain debt of $600 in the hands of the said Lancaster as trustee it being a debt claimed by R. H. GILLIAM the former guardian of the children of Th C LAND in consideration of a certain negro boy GEORGE which was held by the said LAND in right of his wife (who was the widow of the said J. C. GILLIAM) for life and I will hold and apply all or as much of said debt as may not be subject to any claim of LAND, to the benefit of my wards as above named & I do hereby release the said Richard H GILLIAM & his securities as Guardian as aforesaid from all responsibility on account of the said negro boy GEORGE which was sold by the said LAND as aforesaid. As witness my hand & seal this 14th day of January 1851. /signed/ Henry C. THACKSTON, gardian of R. N. Hariott and Ann E. GILLIAM. Witness Alex. MOSELEY.

41. Received Dec 11, 1851 of Richard H. GILLIAM my Guardian $153 as an advance on my legacy that I may be intitled to out of the negroes left myself & brothers & sister by our grandfather Jno. MORGAN and my said Guardian R. H. GILLIAM or his legal representatives are hereby authorized to retain the said amount with interest out of the first money that I may be entitled to in any way, that may come into the said Guardians hand. John W. GILLIAM. Witness. James VIER [his mark]

42. Received Jan 1, 1853 of R. H. GILLIAM Gdn for the heirs of J. D. GILLIAM decd. $15 for keeping SALLY & her four children 1852. William H. COLEMAN.

43. Rock Castle. Appomattox, Jan 5, [18]52
Col Richard H. GILLIAM. Sir.
   Ths. MEGGINSON informed me today that you told him there is a gentleman in the neighbourhood of Buckingham C.[Court] House who wishes to buy a negro woman as cook. Say to him Mother will sell him ANNIE, you know her and will oblige me if you will recommend her to the gentleman. ... Mother will expect the cash for her as her circumstances forces her to sell. Very respectfully in haste.
Lewis H. WINGFIELD
P.S. I wish to make arrangements for you to have your money this year if possible. Eliza WINGFIELD

45. London & Virginia Gold mining Cop.[Company?]
1855. Dr. GLOVER..?
To hire of ZAC 1 month & 11 days at the rate of 200 dollars pr years ...
$23...?
To hire of AARON 2 months at the rate of 45 pr years 7.50

   Interest ?   [Total] 31.50

BONDS, NOTES, LOANS, RECEIPTS

1. John MORRIS - Sir pay Mr. Edward J. GILLIAM $6.50. George T. PYLE. Dec 13, 1824.

2. Rec'd. of R. H. GILLIAM $21.73. 9 Aug 1847. Clifford CABELL.

3. 12 months after date I promise to pay or cause to be paid to Nathan H. THORNTON or order the sum of $2218.23 for true payment of which I bind myself. 1 Dec 1848.

4. Wm. D. JONES Dr. to R. H. GILLIAM. 1840.

5. Due Eliz. G. ANDERSON $200 which I promise to pay on demand. 4 Oct 1848. E. J. GILLIAM.

6. $21.89 On demand with interest from the 1 Jan last I promise to pay to J. & G. B. MOSELEY the sum of 21.89. Joel WATKINS. 14 Dec 1843.

7. On or before 1 June next I promise to pay or cause to be paid to Bryan AKERS $16.00. 11 Aug 1842. Edward J. GILLIAM.

8. Received Dec 1, 1844, $18.50 of R. H. GILLIAM it being the amt. of account of E. GLOVER note on Wm. EVANS. E. J. GILLIAM.

9. To Col. Richard GILLIAM - 11 Aug 1851. My son Lewis will hand you this note with a verbal excuse for my long neglect which misfortune alone has caused you may rest assured that any arrangement he may make with you shall be strictly attended to. E. WINGFIELD.

10. On or before 1 June next I promise to pay John BROWN $10.50. 1 Jan 1835. William FERGUSON, William S. CONNER. Test. Paschal F. MEGLEYNO(?)

11. 12 months after date we promise to pay Thos. H. and A. C. GAR-
NETT, admr. of Wm. GARNETT, dec'd, with interest from date the sum
of 13.25. Mary WHITEHEAD, Powhatan JONES. 11 Nov 1852.

12. Having paid to W. P. BOCOCK $30 and given him my bond for $50 in
all $80 as his fee in my suit now going on in the circuit court of Bucking-
ham against SHORE's admr. it is agreed between us than in case I
recover and make the money he is to have $20 more so as to make $100
in all. Sep 16, 1850. W. P. BOCOCK, James B. FRITWELL.

13. Rec'd of E. G. GILLIAM by the hand of R. H. GILLIAM $6.66 in
full of the balance me for A. A. BALDWIN's bond. ! Apr 1847. E. J. C.
FORBES.

14. Received March 15, 1848. Of Richard H. GILLIAM, admr of Lit-
tlebery HARDIMAN, dec'd, $183 in part of Alexr. FORBES, jr., admr of
Jno. HARDIMAN, which debt was attached in the hand of said Gilliam
as admr. of J. B. HARDIMAN, dec'd. W. W. FORBES assee of Charlotte FORBES, admr.

15. $175. Four months form date I promise to pay to E. B. BENTLY or
order to be paid $175. 22 Feb 1839. R. H. GILLIAM.

16. On demand I promise to pay or cause to be paid to Richard H. GIL-
LIAM or order the sum of $31. 30 Oct 1846. G. W. HENDRECK.

17. On demand I promise to pay Turner H. PATTESON $12.92. 18 Feb
1842. Thos. W. ISBELL. Test. James P. CHRISTIAN.

18. $8.64. On demand I promise to pay to Richard H. GILLIAM $8.64.
7 Sep 1841. James LACKLAND.

19. Colo. R. H. GILLIAM please to pay William LIPSCOMB. $30. Ro.
SHAW. 1 Sep 1851.

20. Borrowed and received of Richard H. GILLIAM. $25. 13 Jan 1844.
John MORGAN.

21. Rec'd. March 25th 1843. of Richard H. GILLIAM $100 in part of his
bond to me for $396.92 as per credit on bond. Thos. W. ISBELL.

22. On bond on Saml. J. WALKER for $101.71 due 7 Oct 1846 on one
John W. ISBELL for $24.61 due 10 ... "Rec'd the above claims of R. H.
GILLIAM for collection by such or otherwise this 9 Apr 184..? Lewis D.
ISBELL.

23. May 28, 1844. Received of Colo. Richard H. GILLIAM by Mr.
GARY a bond for collection by suit executed by Nathl. MORRIS, Saml.
MORRIS and John MORRIS to William M. MOSELEY trustee for sum
of $793.50. 11 Aug 1843. W. P. BOCOCK, by N. F. BOCOCK.

24. Rec'd. Oct 8, 1860 of Richd. H. GILLIAM $20 in part of his note to
me. Tibereous BRYANT.

25. On demand I promise to pay Willis P. BOCOCK on order $300. 14
Sep 1851. R. H. GILLIAM.

26. Received June 11, 1844 of Richard H. GILLIAM, $50.50 in money
and Charles T. BOCOCK note to Th. W. ISBELL for $8.07 which
amounts are to be credited on Th. W. ISBELL's account to me for rent, 1
Jan last. J. T. BOCOCK.

27. On demand I promise to pay Richard H. GILLIAM ... $153. 11 Dec
1851. John H. GILLIAM.

28. Due Nathan H. THORNTON $244.80. 1 Dec 1848. Richard H.
GILLIAM.

29. Capt. Jno. MORGAN to R. H. GILLIAM 1 Jan 1845. $206.97.

30. Dear Col. [R. H. GILLIAM], Lynchburg, Va. 12, 1851. Enclosed I
take the liberty to hand you Rufus C. CHRISTIAN's bond for $14.95 due
2 Sep 1850 which you will please do all in your power to collect for me.
The man I do not know, the debt was made by one of my young men while
he lived in Nelson and ... his circumstance are doubtful. Possibly it may
be ... & ask all full much obliged for your efforts ... me in this collection.
Very respectfully ... Geo. BAGLEY.

SALE OF SAMUEL GREGORY (DECEASED) PROPERTY

Sale of Property belonging to the Estate of Saml. GREGORY Dec'd, made the 15th(?) October 1836.

Saml. WRIGHT, land rented	81.00
William B. COOK, all 10 barrels corn	@4.70
Ditto, nubins @ 2.35	
Benjn. HOOPER, 5000 .. oats	4/6
", 5000	4/6
Benjn. HOOPER, Balance of the oats	4/6
Wm. B. COOK, crop of Tops & shucks	11.00
Tho. O. CLAIBOURNE. 1 large harrow	2.00
R. H. GILLIAM, 1 spinning wheel	3.00
Tho. O. CLAIBOURNE, 1 caster plough	3.80
Barnett HURT, 1 wood till plough	.30
Thos. O. CLAIBOURNE, 1 caster plough	3.85
Martin HURT, 1 double plough	4.00
Martin HURT, 1 small plough	2.75
G. W. KYLE, 1 large ditto	4.05
Martin HURT, 1 large plough, new	3.00
John ROUTON, 1 ditto, ditto, do.	3.25
W. D. JONES, 1 old dagon plough	.25
Nathl. MORRIS, 1 auger &c. ...	3.25
Martin HURT, saw, axe, auger, &c.	2.30
Wm. B. COOKE, 4 axes	3.00
Nathl. MORRIS, lot of tools	1.40
Nathl. MORRIS, lot of hoes	1.25
Tho. O. CLAIBOURNE, ditto, ditto	1.40
W. D. JONES, lot of coulters, grub hoes, &c.	2.90
Martin HURT, saw, draw knife &c.	.45
Zenas SAUNDERS, stretcher	.45 paid
Martin HURT, 4 sythe blades &c.	.55
Nathl. MORRIS, cutting knife	2.80
Danl. MURFEY, ditto	.50
Barnet HURT, 2 sets britching	14.00
Nat. MORRIS, 1 set plough gears 1	.75
ditto, ditto	1.75

Tho. O. CLAIBOURNE, plough gear   1.25
Natl. MORRIS, 2   .05
Danl. MURFEY, 1 grind stone   1.50
Barnet HURT, 1 still cap & worm   1.25
W. D. JONES, 1 bell   .25
M. REYNOLDS, 1 wine barrel   .50
Barnet HURT, 1 waggon   13.00
Barnet HURT, 1 ox cart   13.00
Barnet HURT, 1 yoke oxen   38.00
Barnet HURT, 1 ditto, ditto   31.00
B. HURT, 1 log chain   2.00
Mrs. GREGORY, 1 pan   .25
Barnet HURT, 2 set spools &c. coffee mill   .30
Edmd. GREGORY, 2 cut wheel and foot wheel   .30
Edward W. CURD, brindles, basket, tonge, &c.   1.75
W. D. JONES, brass skillet, pot rack, &c.   .95
Barnet HURT, lot of pots   .55
Jonas EAGLES, bed and furniture   10.00
Barnet HURT, 1 ditto, ditto   9.00
Mrs. WRIGHT, 1 pine chest   .65
William WARRINER, 1 walnut chester   .75 paid
William WARRINER, 1 cupboard, walnut   2.00
W. D. JONES, parcel of chairs (5)   .31
         2 looking glasses   .37
Mrs. [Ann] GREGORY, 1 table and contents   .50
B. HURT, 1 saddle   3.00
Wm. TOPP, 1 Red Heifer   10.80
Goodrick SANDERS, red steer   12.05
Chas. MCKENNEY, 1 red cow   16.50
David BONDURANT, 1 milk and ... heifer   10.00
Jonas EAGLES, 1 cow and calf   16.00
Sml. WRIGHT, 2 yearlings   9.00
Alfred CHILDERS, not delivered on as a shoe gun of not giving
security   6.25
William B. COKEE [Cooke], 1 stack with the privilege of the whole 3/
Saml. WRIGHT, 1 sow & pigs   5.00

HARDIMAN ESTATE

Littlebury HARDIMAN late of the county of Buckingham, Va. dec'd, dying without will and whereas Thomas HARDIMAN late of the County of Giles, TN, and brother of said Littlebury HARDIMAN being dead, therefore know ye that we Anderson HARDIMAN son of the said Thomas HARDIMAN, dec'd and Samuel SMITH and Nace E. DAVIDSON who married daughters of the said Thomas HARDIMAN, dec'd claim in right of their wives Judith SMITH and Luzany DAVIDSON wives of the said Samuel SMITH and Nace E. DAVIDSON and daughters of said Thomas HARDIMAN, dec'd (who are the lawful heirs of the said Littlebury HARDIMAN. Anderson HARDIMAN son of said Thomas HARDIMAN, dec'd and Samuel SMITH and Mace E. DAVIDSON who claim in right of their wives... appoint John E. HARDIMAN of the county of Giles, state of TN our atty and demand from said Richard H. GILLIAM the legacy ...

Decree of County court of Buckingham pronounced on 13 Dec 1847 in a suit depending in the said court between Lawson G. TYLER and Elizabeth his wife pltfs [plaintiffs] and Richard H. GILLIAM admr of Littlebury HARDIMAN, dec'd and others defendants it was ordered and decreed that John MORRIS, Grandison MOSELY, John J. GILLIAM, Tandy HOLEMAN and Moses A. SPENCER or any three of them should divide the slaves of Littlebury HARDIMAN, dec'd and all allot to William W. DEVENPORT admr of Charles HARDIMAN, dec'd 1/9 part..., John HARDIMAN 1/9 part.

John HARDIMAN, Robertson Co., TN, for love and affection which I entertain for my dau Harriett HARDIMAN of Co and state aforesaid, all right to the estate of my brother Littlebury HARDAMAN, dec'd late of Buckingham Va.

I Harriatt HARDYMAN of Robertson, TN nominate my brother Samuel HARDYMAN of state and co. aforesaid as my atty.

I William H. ROBERTSON, husband of Elizabeth ROBERTSON, dau of William HARDIMAN, myself of the co. of Scott, Mississippi, appoint Bibzer HARDEMAN of Oglethorp Co, GA. atty to recover ... estate of Berry HARDIMAN, now dec. ...

MILITIA FINES

At a Regimental Court of inquiry held for the 100 Regiment on the 12th
day of November 1842 at Robert MOORE's in the County of Buckingham It was ordered that the Sheriff of Buckingham County have credit for
the following.

Tickets, Muster fines remitted

Pleasant A. COBBS	.75
Jesse A. CARTER	2.25
Robert COLEMAN	1.50
John MATTHEWS	2.25
Patrick PAMPLIN	2.25
John STINSON	2.25
Thomas F. WRIGHT	.75
James B. WILKERSON	.75
Stephen D. DAVIDSON	.75
Nathaniel GUILL	.75
Benjamin WORD	.50
Tandy MATTHEWS	.75
Edmund TINDALL	1.50
Charles HARDIMAN	1.50
John W. HARDIMAN	1.50

Benjamin H. MORRIS fined for not attending Regimental & October
Musters 1843 in Capt. PATTESON's Company 150 cents. Wm. D.
CHRISTIAN, CCE.

William BONDURANT fined for not attending Extra ... July 1844 in
Capt. DAVIS's company. H. A. LEGON, Clk.

Archibald B. MEGGINSON fined for not attending April Regimental &
October Musters 1842 in Capt. NOWLIN's compy - 228 cents. W. D.
CHRISTIAN CCE.

LIST OF TICKETS TO BE COLLECTED

Rcd of R. H. GILLIAM [this] list of tickets to collect according to law.
W. H. THORNTON, D [Deputy] for Jno. MORRIS, Shff. Aug 12 1840.

Muster fines in 100th Regt.

AUSTIN, Jas. Jr .	2.25
BURTEN, Robert	.75
COBBS, Watson B.	.75
COBBS, Thomas	.75
ELDRIDGE, Benjn.	.75
GOUGH, Wm.	.75
HASKINS, Jno. W.	.75
WEST, Benjn.	.75
WORD, Benjn.	.75
TINDELL, Jno.	.75

Comm. of Revenues	
OVETIN & BLAND	.75
~~PERKINS Thos. H~~	~~.75~~
Porhouse	.75
LIGHTFOOT, Jno.	.75
IRVING, H. & Jos.	.75
GARY, Jno. Est	.50
CHRISTIAN, Chs. L.	.75
Clerk AMHERST	
D. BOATWRIGHT[?]	1.00

POOR HOUSE OF BUCKINGHAM COUNTY

At a stated meeting of the overseers of the poor for the county of Buckingham held at the poor house of said county on monday 6 July 1846.

Ordered that the salary of the physician for the present year be fixed at $40 and that the collector pay the same. Ordered that David KYLE be appointed physician for the ensuing year.

Ordered that the collector for the last year be charged with 5769 levies at 33 cents. $1903.77

cr. By Nathl. MORRIS list of insolvents	$42.57
cr. by Wm. P. OLIVERS list of insolvents	40.26
cr. by Wm. W. FORBES list of insolvents	54.78
cr. by this sum paid Supt. salary	250.00
cr. by this sum paid John A. LANCASTER	1.20
cr. by George RUSH	3.00
cr. by Robert A. PHELPS	13.50
cr. by Wilson HIX	6.25
cr. by overseers of the poor Prince Edward County	8.00
cr. by Edward J. GILLIAM	5.00
cr. by Wm. W. WRIGHT	4.00
cr. by John NEWTON	3.00
cr. Saml. B. CHRISTIAN	11.25
cr. by Nathan A. HOLEMAN	1.13
cr. by John S. WEST & Co.	1.41
cr. by Benjamin D. ANDERSON	37.25
cr. by David KYLE	53.00
cr. by this sum paid Supt., general assee	1300.00.
cr. by this sum paid overseers of the poor	30.00.
commission on 1766:40 at 6 per cent	105.96.
	1971.56

Balance due the shff. $67.79

Ordered that the salary of the superintendent be fixed at $250 for the ensuing year, and that the collector pay the same, ordered that Miles GIPSON be appointed superintendent and clerk for the ensuing year.

ORDERED that John MORRIS sheriff of Buckingham be appointed collector for the next year.

ORDERED that the collector pay D. Clifford CABELL $4 for a barrel of flour furnished Martin BRYANT.

ORDERED that the collector pay Nicholas & brothers .75 for six pounds of bacon furnished to B. BOATWRIGHT.

ORDERED that the collector pay HOLEMAN & HARRIS $13.125 for medical services rendered Betty BOATWRIGHT.

ORDERED that the collector to Stephen GARROTT $1.00 and Nathan A. HOLEMAN $1 for provisions furnished Mrs. Francis OLIVER.

ORDERED that the collector pay Robert K. HOCKER .93 for articles furnished Mrs. CRIDDLE.

ORDERED that the collector pay George W. MCKINNEY for the benefit of James CRANK &Co. $1.25 for articles furnished Betty BOATWRIGHT..

ORDERED the collector pay Bashaba GARROTT $2 for attendance on Judith AMOS as midwife.

ORDERED that the collector pay Edward REES $2 for wood furnished Rhoda SCOTT.

ORDERED that the collector pay to David KYLE $10 for medical service rendered Kitty SCOTT and Mrs. BLUNDLE.

ORDERED that the collector pay Saml. B. CHRISTIAN $10 for medical services rendered Amanda GODSAY.

ORDERED that the collector pay John A. LANCASTER $3.96 for articles furnished Lydia GODSEY and Polley HARVEY.

ORDERED that the collector pay LEWIS and PATTESON $2.18 for articles for shroud for Mrs. WILLIAMS.

ORDERED that the collector pay ALLEN and PHAUP $3 for articles furnished Mr. SPROUSE and Mrs. EDWARDS.

ORDERED that the collector pay George HOCKER $2.50 for half barrel corn for Mr. SPROUSE.

ORDERED that the collector pay to Roland SPROUSE $20 towards his support to be paid quarterly.

ORDERED that the collector pay to Mourning WHITLER $12 toward her support.

ORDERED that the collector pay to Matthew A. COX $42 for board and attention to James GRIGGS while sick at his house.

On motion the order allowing Mourning WHITLER $12 was reconsidered and upon reconsideration was rejected.

The balance due the shff. of Buckingham brought ford. $67.79

Hugh ROBERTSON returned non resident 2 levies   .66

$68.45

To Anderson INGLE improperly credited   .33

$68.12

ORDERED that the collector be charged with five thousand 5 hundred and eighty one tythes at 35 cents.

ORDERED that the collector pay to the superintendent $1200 for general account of expenses.

ORDERED that the collector pay Wm. MOSELEY, Frederick SCRUGGS, James WOODFIN, Thomas M. BONDURANT, James M. PATTISON, John M. HARRIS, Edward J. GILLIAM, Dr. Clifford CABELL, Cary H. McCRAW, Alexander MOSELEY, Quin M. WORD, and Philip A. BOLLING $1 each for their attendance to day and that the further sum of $1 be paid James M. PATTISON for attendance one day last year, also one dollar to Ambrose FORD, and two dollars to Cary H. McCRAW for two days attendance since the last meeting. A copy M. GIPSON, clk. O/P [Overseers of the Poor]

SCHOOLS (TEACHERS, SCHOOL TAXES, TUITION)

Cash paid Paschal JONES	27.36
S. E. ROBERT	10.20
Miss MUNSON	16.76
A. MAXEY	17.69
M. LEWIS	15.75
Chs. T. BOCOCK	8.25
96.01	

Jno. SPENCER	90.49
Jno. S. PATTESON	58.39
N. A. HOLEMAN	6.05
Alfred JORDEN	13.12
	264.06
Amt. brt. forward	264.06
John H. HARVEY	12.25
Saml. BRIGHTWELL	42.42
R. SAUNDERS	19.70
J. H. SISAN	88.29
	426.72
Mary J. GILLS	13.00
John STINSON	13.96
Jno. FITZGERALD	25.76
Chs. DAVIDSON	6.27
Mary CHRISTIAN	26.02
Wm. D. CHRISTIAN	47.44
	559.17
Emeline EANS(?)	12.
	571.17
Jno. R. WILLIAMS	2.50
	573.67

Rec'd 1st January 1843.

Of Richd. H. GILLIAM $26.02 in full of Miss Mary B. CHRISTIAN's account for the tuition of poor children allowed by the board October 1842 - for which I have an order from Miss M. B. CHRISTIAN but have misplaced it. Turner H. PATTESON.

Miss Mary B. CHRISTIAN

To the Treasurer of the School fund for Buckingham County Dr.

To cash paid Turner H. PATTESON amt his tax 1842 $20.41

To cash paid bal. of Jas. P. CHRISTIAN's tax 1842 2.74

23.15

Cash paid Turner H. PATTESON 2.87

26.02

By amt. of our account for the tuition of poor children   26.02

May 25, 1843. Colo. R. H. GILLIAM, Sir, on sight pay to Th. PARRACK the sum of $46.30 his claim against the S. C. for the tuition of poor children in the year 1843. James MERIDETH, S. C.

Colo. Richard GILLIAM. In A/c with Henry T. MEREDITH dr. Dec 15th to Tuition of Richard S. GILLIAM for 5 20/30 mo.at $2 pr mo. $11.33 1/3.

1856 Sep 10. Mr. Richard GILLIAM in a/c with W. D. DAVIS prescription for your .... (at F. C. [Female College] Institute) $1.00

Due 1 Jany 1857

TAX ASSESSMENTS

1. Sept. 22d, 1825 - Edward GILLIAM. 1825 one levy, 1 horse

2. 1836 - Saml. GREGORY's Est. To land 68, 7 slaves & 3 horses 1.90, 6 levies - $7.86. Recd. payment of Richd. H. Gilliam admr of Saml. Gregory decd.

3. S. B. MEGGERSON - Tax on land $24, 1 Blacks 1 horse 1.43, 2 tithes.

4. 1840 - Allen WOODY. To 6 Blacks, 1 horse - 1.88, 7 tithes - 3.85. $5.73.

5. 1841 - Elizabeth CONNER. 1 slave, 1 horse - .53; 2 levies - 1.38. $1.91. Land tax for Est Jas. CONNER 1.01. $2.02

6. 1842. Mr. Saml. BURKS. To 1 horse .3. To County and Parish Levies .70. To Sundry Tickets rendered Due bill 3.57. $4.40

7. Francis McFADDEN. 1 slave .46. Tax 1842 1.80. 2 levies 1.24.

Tickets. 3.50.

8. 1842. Mr. Wm. H. MATHEWS. To 2 slaves and 5 horses & Barrouche ...[obliterated. 3 county and parish levies 2...? Sundry tickets rendered - 20.00. $25.50.

9. Mr. Francis LAND. 1842 Tax on land. .17. 1 slave and 1 horse .53. 1 do and 1 do. 53 c & 1 levy for 1841 1.22. 1 county and Parish levys .70. Tickets rendered .75. $3.37.

10. Mr. Charles SMITH. 1842 To 1 slave and 1 horse.53, 2 county and parish levies 1.40. 1 horse and 2 levies (for 1841) 1.50. $3.43.

11. Est. Jno. C. BROWN. 1843 - Land .60. Do for 1841 and 1842 1.00. $1.60.

12. Mr. Samuel L. BURKS. 1843 To 1 slave, 1 horse - .60. To 1 levies - .62. To Tax 1842 - 3.30. $4.52.

13. Mr. Frd.[?] N. CABELL Trustee for E. W. CABELL. 1843 - To land 16.17, to 5 slaves, 2 horses - 2.58; to 3 levies 1.86; to Tickets $17.89. $38.50.

14. Mr. H. FERGUSON. 1843 - To land for est D. FERGUSON 5.40; to 2 slaves, 2 horses, m. clock & 1 gold watch - 2.70. To 3 levies - 1.86; to Tickets (Bal 1842). $5.14.

15. Mrs. Frances LAND. 1843 to land .20; to 1 slave, 2 horses .74. To 2 levies 1.24; 2 use[?] as admrs of A. LAND 1.50. $3.68.

16. Mr. Saml. B. MEGGINSON. 1843 to 1 slave, 1 horse .60. To 1 levy - .62. To tickets, .36, .75 1.11. $2.33.

17. Mr. Benja. S. MORRIS. 1843 - To land for R. G. & Jno. MORRIS .90. To 4 slaves, 7 horses & W. Clock 3.07. To 4 levies 2.48. To Tickets - 6.08. $12.53.

18. Mr. Chas. SMITH. 1843 - To 1 horse, 1 levy .76. Amt for 1842 payt. 3.43. $4.19.

19. Catharine WILLIAMS. 1843 - To Lot in Bent Creek .08. [remainder obliterated]

20. Frederick M. CABELL Trustee E. W. CABELL. 1844 - To land 13.47; 5 slaves and 3 horses 2.38; 3 levies 1.50. Tax 1843 pr account 41.96. Tickets 5.86. $65.17. By Cash of R. ELDRIDGE 20.00. $45.17

21. Saml. B. MEGGINSON. 1844 - To 1 slave and 1 horse .53. 2 levies 1.00. Balance Tax 1843 - .75. $2.28.

22. Mr. Benjamin S. MORRIS. 1844 to land .52; 3 slaves, 3 horse W. Clock 1.83; 3 levies 1.50. Tax 1843 per account 12.53. Tickets 13.73. Muster fine 1.50. By County Levy 20.00. Bal. 11.01

23. Mr. Archibald B. MEGGERSON. 1844 - To land 4.79; 14 slaves, 13 horses and W. Clock 7.48; 13 levies 6.50. Muster fine 1843 2.25. Tickets 4.00. Tax on decd from D.C. JONES, Saml. J. WALKER & Wm. WALTON & wife .50. Tax on decd from D. C. JONES, Wm. WALTON & wife, Saml. MCDEASMON & S. J. WATKINS .50. $26.02.

24. Mr. David PRYOR Est. 1844 - Land .09. Land 1841, 42, 43 -.29. $.38

25. Mr. Charles SMITH. 1 horse, 1 levy .63. Amo. for 1843 p a/c 4.19. $4.82.

26. Samuel J. WALKER. 1844 to land - 15.16; 29 slaves, 16 horses, coach M. C. & 2 G. Watches 18.35; 28 levies 14.00. Bal: tax 1843 40...? Tax on Jonathan, P. PHELPS will - .50. Tax on decd from Jno. JOHNS & wife - .50. Tax on decd from Wm. WALTON - .50. Tickets 16.29. $105.37.

27. Mr. Frs. AMOS Est. 1845 - To tax on 440 land - .22. 1846 440 a. land .22. $.44.

28. Mr. Thos. AUSTIN. 1845 - to 1 county and parish levy .83

29. Est. John D. BROWN. Land .50. Tax 1843 per account 1.60. $2.10.

30. Mr. Saml. BUCKS. 1845 - 1 horse - .10. To county and parish levies - .83. To sundry tickets rendered - 6.35. $7.28.

31. William F. BONDURANT. 1845 - To tax on land 1.87. Tax on 5 slaves, 3 horses, bar & w. Clock 4.35. Levies 8 - 6.64. M. Fine - .50. $13.10.

32. Mr. H. B. CASON. 1845 - To tax on 1 horse - .10. 1 wood clock - .13. To sundry Tickets rendered - 1.26. $1.49.

33. FERGUSON, David H. 1845 - Tax on 4 B, 1 horse, 1 gw., 1 w clock 2.63. 5 tithes - 5.00.

34. Mr. William H. MATTHEWS. 184. - 2 horses & wood clock - .53. 2 levies - 1.24. Tickets - 10.47. $12.24.

35. Mr. Jno. P. PITTMAN. 1845. 1 levy - .83; sundry tickets .66. $1.49.

36. Mr. Wm. RAKES. 1845. 1 slave - .32; 1 levy - .83. $1.15.

37. Mr. Abraham STRATTON. 1845. Tax on land - .10. 1 horse [unclear but total is 4.42].

38. Nancy WADE. 1845. To tax on land for est Wm. Wade ?? To tax on 2 slaves for ...??? 1 levy for Geo. Wade ...?? 1 levy for Fr...?? 2 levies...??

39. ... WADE Est[ate]. 150 land - .38. 1 slave - .32. 1 levy 1.20. Sundry tickets rendered - 4.70. $6.60.

40. Mr. A. AUSTIN. 1846. To tax on 25 land - .10. 1 levy - 1.20. Sundry tickets rendered - 1.07. $2.37.

41. Mr. Th AUSTIN. 1846. 1 levy - 1.20. Sundry tickets rendered - .83. $2.03.

42. Mr. Hiram B. CASON. 1846. Wood clock - .13. 1 levy - 1.20. Sundry tickets rendered 1.49. $2.82.

43. Mr. John CHENAULT. 1846. 1 slave, 1 horse - .42. 2 levies - 2.40. $2.82.

44. Jas. CONNERS Est. 1846. 200 land - .20. 1 slave, 1 horse for E. Conner - .42. Tax 1845 - .30. 1 levy 1.20.

45. Jas. CREWS. 1846. Tax on s. watch 1845 .25 1 levy and s watch 1.45. $1.70.

46. Jas. M. FALKNER. 1 w. clock .25.

47. Mr. Jno. & Jos. FIZJERALD. 1 horse - .10. 1 horse 1845 - .10. 1 s watch per Jos. .25. 2 levies 2.40. $2.85.

48. Wm. F. GIBSON. 1846. 1 levy - 1.20.

49. Wm. HARRIS. 1846. 25 acres. $.13.

50. Jno. HORSLEY. 1846. 1100 acres. $1.10.

51. Mrs. Lucy A. HUNDLEY. 1846. 38 acres. $.12.

52. Mrs. Sally McFADDEN. 1846. 30 acres, 1 levy (for son Wm.). $1.28.

53. Creed KITCHIN. 1846. 33 1/3 acres. $.07.

54. John H. KITCHIN. 1846. 33 1/3 acres plus land tax for 1845. $.14.

55. Wm. B. KITCHIN. 1846. 33 1/3 acres ($.07), 1 horse, ($.10), 50 acres for E. KITCHIN ($.14), Old land tax (on Elijah KITCHIN's land - $1.05), 1 levy ($1.20). $2.56.

56. Gabriel LAYNE. 1846. [Acreage not given] $.35.

57. Mrs. Judeth B. PATTESON. 1846. 125 acres. $.19.

58. Jno. P. PITTMAN. 1846. 1 horse (.10), 1 levy, sundry tickets (50 + 1.05). $2.85.

59. Wm. T. PRYOR. 1846. 61 acres (.07), Land (1841, 42, 43, 44 & 45 - .40) $.47.

60. Richd. RAGLAND. 1846. 24 acres ($.12), 1 horse ($.10), 1 levy. $1.42.

61. Mrs. Ann RAKES. 1846. 80 acres ($.08), Land in 1845 ($.08). $.16.

62. Benja. RAKES. 1846. 102 1/2 acres ($.21), 1 levy ($1.21). $1.42.

63. Mrs. Elizabeth & Jno. RAKES. 1846. 56 acres ($.12), Land tax 1845 ($.12). $.24.

64. Henry RAKES. 1846. 202 acres (for Wilson Branch). $.61.

65. Wm. RAKES Est[ate]. 1846. 474 acres ($1.43), tax for 1845 ($1.15). $2.58.

66. Charles SMITH. 1846. 1 horse ($.10), 1 levy, sundry tickets rendered (5.13). $6.43.

67. Benj. & Saml. VEST 1846. 1 horse ($.10), 2 levies. $2.50.

TICKET LISTS

Tickets to the clerk of Buckingham received by R. H. Gilliam in 1843.

Agee, Jas. M. 5.34
Abbell. Wms. orphans .36
Austin, Bernard for..? .54
Austin, Archd. .41
Austin, Archer's exs. 1.14
Abbell, Geo. 1.50
Anderson, Lawrence 10.08
Th. Austin 10.08
Agee, Th. ...? 5.47
Bryant Jno. B. 1.50
Brown for R. G. Morris 1.50
Burks Jos. 3.58
Baskerville, Mary .37
Bocock, J. T. .58
Beckley, Jos's (Guardn.) 1.21
Bocock W. P. & J. H. S... 1.00
Bocock W. P. & T. S. 3.00
Branch, Wilson 1.95
Bibb, Henry 1.50
Bibb, Geo. W. 2.49
W. P. & T. S. Bocock, trustees 2.45
Bollings trustees Bocock 2.42
Do, Do 3.88
Bock, trust. for J. H. S... 3.87
Bell, P. B. 1.62
B..., Thos. Orphans .36
B..., Thos. Andr. 2.46
Cason, Fugua 1.50
Conner, John's admr. 3.52
Carnifix, Mary's admr. 1.73
Conner, Chas.' Exr 1.00
Chick, Wm. 3.60

Casson, Jas. W. 1.50
Cabell, Clifford 1.50
Cabell, T. M. 3.89
Christian, Stephen 3.98
Christian, Wm. D. 9.31
Flood, J.W. .58
Ferguson, Bartlet, admr. 1.00
Flood & Trent for Watkins 1.58
Ferguson Wm. G. 1.50
Fanss (Farris?), Jas. 3.91
Ferguson, Wm. U. .54
Fitzpatrick, Nicholas, admr. 3.46
Flood, ...? 1.50
Flood, H. D. 3.00. Do .54
Flood, T. H.1.16
Flood & Nowlin 10.12
Flood, Th. H. 5.91
Flood & Trent 6.23
Ferguson Wm. W. D. 26.66
Evans & Cook for B. Mooris 1.58
Deane, Jas. T. .54
Davidson, Judith .37
Deane, Jas. T. .50
Doss, Jno's Exr. .73
Dunn, Wm. J. 1.99
Dillard, Jos. S. 1.50
Davidson, Jno. H. 3.10
Horsley, Jno. .18
Harris, Jno's admr 1.80
Hardiman, Geo. W. 2.43
Hardiman, Sam. B. 4.90
Hammer, Jas. A. 3.00

Hix, Wilson for &c. 2.49
Hix, Wilson. 22.49
Gipson, Polly 1.80
Goodwin, Jas. .41
Gordon, Obd. .41
Glover, Eliz. for &c. 4.07
Gilliam, R. H. 5.25
Gooch & Cheatwood for &c 10.47
Linthicum, Ed & C. 1.42
Layne, Sam. S. assn. 1.57
Linthicum, Henry .18
Do, trustee 1.50
Kitchin, Wm. .18
Kitchin, Wm. A. .41
Kyle, H. C. 2.12
Johnson, Washtn. .18
Isbell, Th. U. .68
Jennings, Bint.(?) .40
Jennings, Jesse 1.06
Jones, W. B., trustee 1.50
Jennings, Ben. W. 1.50
Johnson, Thos. 2.17
Johnson, Richd. senr. 1.80
Johnson, Richd. 1.50
Isbell, Lewis D. 3.71
Johnson, Jno. H. 2.33.
Jones Wm. B. 1.50
Jones, Eliz. 1.92
Jones, Josias 3.58
Johnson, Jno. H. 4.20
Overton, Jas. W. 1.50
Oakes, Major 2.75
North, Chas..36
North, Ant. A. .55
Nowlin, Bryant 4.59
North, Anthony 1.50

Miles, Chas. 1.78
Moseley, Va. R. .58
Moore, Ben. A. .72
Moore, Wm. .36
Megginson, Jos.' admr. .48
McFadin, Jer. tus? 1.50
Moore, Wm. .18
McFaden, Jer. .18
Megginson, Sam. B. .36
Megginson, Jos. C. .68
Megginson, Wm. W.(?).18
Moseley, Gr. trust. 1.50
McFaden, Jer. 1.50
Moseley, R. E. 1.24
Moore, Wm. 1.80
Matthews, Jno. &c. 1.30
Megginson, Jno. R. 1.24
McFadin, Martha & Wm. 1.50
Moore, Robt. 2.72
Matthews, Wm. H. 7.28
Moseley, Ro. E. Sp. 10.82
Moseley Wm. P. 10.14
Morris, R. G. 13.20
Moseley, Wm. 18.07
Pattison, Wm. 23.49
Pattison, Turner H. .18
Phelps, Peter W. .40
Patteson, Jas. admr. .36
Pankey, Jas. &c. .59
Pattison, Ben & Robt. .62
Phelps, Robt. .80
Phelps, Anna 1.50
Phelps, Nelson .84
Phelps, Joseph 1.50
Phelps, J. P. & S J. Wacker 2.82
Phelps, Jas. (s ch) 4.76

Palmer, Isbell &c. 1.50
Phelps, Wm. E. 1.50
Pattison, Wm. for &c. 1.50
Palmore, Jos. admr. 2.04
Pettecrew, Wm. & Mat. .41
Pettecrew, Mat. 1.13
Phelps, Alexr's exr. 3.15
Palmer, R. D. 4.58
Pankey, Peter B., guardn. 4.34
Phelps, Jas. (WJ?) 4.68
Perkins,W. H. Est. 4.37
Perkins, Th. T. 7.20
Plunket, Ambrose 5.16
Pankey, Jno. 7.62
Phelps, Jon. P. 15.32
Phelps, Ro. P., admr 10.93
Reynolds, Isaac 4.07
Robinson, Jas' admr. 2.26
Reves & White 3.40
Robinson, Hugh D. .36
Reynolds, Francis 1.35
Sea...?, Coleman 1.50
Staples & Gary 1.56
Stell, Wm. 2.00
Salle, Isaac for Bock. .54
Stalkum, Jas. Guardn. 1.25
Stell, Wm. H. 1.50
Stephens, Absalom 1.50
Spencer. Wm. 1.50. Ditto 2.84
Spencer, Jno. R. 3.85
Stinson, Jno. 2.22
Stinson, Geo. 2.67
Wright, Wm. .18
Wingfield, Tho. .18
Wackens, Phil .18
Walker, Ben .36

Wright, David .40
Warriner, David's admr. .85
Wall, Jas' admr. .40
Webb, Abram M. .59
Webb, Martin .81
Webb, Wm. admr. 1.33
Wright, Jno. M. 1.60
Wright, Tho. P. 1.50
Woodson, Drury 1.10
Webb, Merry 1.50
Wingfield, Tho. 1.41
Wright, Tho. P. 1.32
Woodson, Drury 1.50
Walker, Ben P. 1.91
Walker, Gabl. 1.50
White, And. trustee 1.50
Watkins, Joel & H. P. 2.64
White, And. trustee 2.80
Woodroof's, exr. &c. 1.96
Webb, Merry for &c. 2.16
Watson, Jas. admr 2.04
Webb, Wm's exr. 4.68
Woodson, Tarlton(?) H. 3.56
Wingfield, Mat. &c. 5.38
White, And. 1.44
Walker, Saml. J. 4.99
Watkins, Joel 3.88
Wright, Thos', exr. 7.58
Thomas, Chas. .36
Tyler, Chas. 36
Taylor, A. H. & wife 1.50
Thornhill, Wm. jr. 1.50
Trent, Thos., trustee 1.50
Trent, Jno. 1.30
Thornhill, Eliz.' admr. 4.07
Trent, Thos. 19.40

"Record August 18th 1843. Of William M. Mosely the foregoing list of tickets from the clerk of Buckingham. [on one whole sheet and a part of this} for collection. Rh. Gilliam."

S. Mathews to Sundries For F. Mathews.

Due 1 Sept. 1832.

Robt. S. Andrews 36.43

L. G. Brown 238.96

L. G. Brown, Grd. of C. Wood .25

Benjamin Boatright 36.69

John B. Baker 37.50

Mr. Andrew Baker 8.81

J. T. & J. R. Cheedle 321.97

Benjamin Cox 2.75

Margaret Davis 41.50

Peter Davis 17.52

Sam. C. Fore 93.22

Thomas Giles 82.99

Josiah Giles 51.27

John Lippord 121.66

Anderson J. Lovern 18.39

Thomas Mosley 210.82

Johnson Mcneed 6.05

James Martin 324.58

Tarlton Mathews 355.08

Joel E. Mickle 10.99

Marcus P. McGlasson 58.63

Ralph Merryman 18.32

Banister S. Pryor 118.91

Wm. H. Porter 3.84

Richard P. Richardson 3.01

Doct. Begin Snell 52.04

Nathaniel Wilkerson 101.40

Capt. Joseph Wilson 80.24

Sam Walker 31.18

Philip Watkins 39.92

Robt. Wilkerson 3.12

Richard Woodson 104.14

George & Merry Webb 103.52

Abner Watson 1.25

David Walker 34.88

J. H. & W. Wilson 537.08

Thomas Grubb 18.82

Isaih Lewis 34.30

Claibron Harris 23.15

William J. Moon 26.35

Sarah Grubb 5.39

Archibald R. Brightwell 9.85

John Ransone 2.76

Obadiah Gorden .50

E. M. W. Durphy 1.90

John B. Davis 17.83

Wm. Brightwell, snr. 9.95

Charles Farrow 11,76

Josiah Mosley 13.71

Henry W. Holland 150.58

Chas. Mckiny, Grd of Perry Watkins 20.18

Chas. McKiny, Grd of Rhoda Watkins 53.23

Chas. McKiny, Grd of Jas. Watkins 4.81

Chas. McKiny, Grd of Susan Watkins 11.92

Edward Watkins 42.32

Sam H. Cunningham 112.80

Amos Lifford 39.32

Wm. W. Thackston 127.76

John T. Linthicum 12.75

Pugh Price 2.50

Garland Anderson 53.63
Sarah Moore 58.95
Charles Woodson 188.57
Martha Price 4.18

Wm. D. Taylor 6.12
Thomas Burnett 82.64
Joshua Whirley 7.05
Benjamin Giles 6.45

ACCOUNTS

Horses, carriages, gigs, wagons

1. 1825, 10 Oct. Rec'd of Edward J. GILLIAM, $160.00 for a gigg. Saml. HIX.

2. 1844, 6 Aug. Rec'd of R. H. GILLIAM, $20.00 for a one-horse waggon sold him. Thos. MILLER.

3. Col. R. H. GILLIAM acct. with A. D. CHOCKLEY.
1851: 1 collar (1.25), repairing harness (3.50), 1 double girth (1.25), 1 reine (.50), mending briddle (.13), 1 saddle (22.00), 1 cloth (1.00).
1851, 5 Jan - Credit: by 10 1/2 bushells wheat @65 (6.82)
1852: 1 pr. bays (6.50), 1 mastingale? fr. Davidson (1.25), 1 pr. carriage lines (5.00), 2 mastingale? (1.50).
1853: 1 briddle filling (1.75), 2 collars (2.50).
Rec'd payment on settlement on 5 Apr 1853 - $32.31.

4. 1853, 30 June.   R. H. GILLIAM - Bot. of Alfred KING 1 carriage and Harness - $600.00.

5. 1854, 18 Nov. Received of Henry R. JOHNSON by the hand of Rich. H. GILLIAM, fifty dollars in full for one old Horse sold him. Thos. H. PERKINS.

6. 1862, 25 Nov. Rec'd. of Col. R. H. GILLIAM one Hundred Dollars for a horse. Thomas MCKINNEY.

7. 1875, 12 April. Received of R. H. GILLIAM one hundred dollars in full for the purchase of a dark mare, 5 years old. R. C. APPLING, Gap Mills, Monroe Co., W. Va.

Coffins and Burial Articles

1. 1836, 23 May. Mr. Samuel GREGORY estate to George RUSH: one coffin (15.00), to carrying the corps to the grave (2.00).

2. 1849, 19 Sep. Mr. Richard H. GILLIAM to Elizabeth TYLER. Debit 1847 to the binding the shroud and winding sheet for Littleberry HARDIMAN to be buried in. $5.00. Rec'd. in full - Lawson TYLER.

3. 1850. Mr. Richard H. GILLIAM in acct. with DAVIS & WORD: making coffin and case for Mrs. GILLIAM (20.00).

4. 1855, 30 July. Col. R. H. GILLIAM to George W. CLAIBOURNE: To making coffin for child (10.00). Rec'd payment - George W. CLAIBOURN by John P. PERKINSON.

5. 1861, 11 Feb. Received of Col. Richard H. GILLIAM $33.00 in full for coffin for his wife last Sept. James DAVIS.

6. 1875, 26 March. Estate of Capt. E. J. GILLIAM, debt to J. M. ANDERSON: To making burial cage (7.00). On back of receipt: coffin (7.00), Alpacker for covering (1.50), Cambrick for lining (1.50), Shroud (1.50). [Total: $12.00]

Shoes

1. 1843, 24 Nov. To Col. Ricd. H. GILLIAM by Allen. Sir: Allen has made 16 sixteen stitchdown shoes - $8 an half pair - I think they are good shoes - concequently, I am well pleased - so far - Yours Respectfully. S. P. HARDWICKE [Samuel P. Hardwicke]

2. R. H. Gilliam, in acct. with Thomas PARRACK:

1849: 1 pair boots (6.50), repairing boots (4.50), repairing shoes (.50), making 4 pair shoes (1.00).

1850: repairing boots (6.75), repairing shoes (2.75), making 2 pr. shoes for Miss GILLIAM (2.50).

3. 1849, 20 Dec. R. H. GILLIAM, adm. of John D. GILLIAM, dec. To Tarlton P. LEWIS: to making 3 pairs shoes for three boys @ .30 (.90).

004. 1864, 25 Nov. Col. R. H. GILLIAM, gurdin [guardian] for John D. GILLIAM, children in acct. with R. J. DAVIS: to 1 pair shoes (1.25). Rec'd payment, 6 June 1854 - Wm. S. WISE, adm of R. J. DAVIS, dec.

Tailoring

1. 1846. Mr. Richard H. GILLIAM in acct. with Peter SIPE: making Jenny coat (3.50), cutting pants (.25), cutting coat pattern (.25). 2. 1850. R. G. GARY, To Peter SIPE: making vest & pants (3.00), repairing coat (1.00), making vest & pants (3.00).

3. 1852. Col. R. H. GILLIAM in acct. with Peter SIPE: cutting, trimming pants (1.00), cash paid Mrs. GREGORY for making pair of fine pants (9.00), one fine coat & vest (30.00), cutting pants (.50), making James coat (4.50), cash paid H. STERN for two pair drawers (3.00), one fine silk vest & black pants (19.00), one fine frock coat (27.00), fine stock (1.50).

4. 1858, 12 May. Mrs. Mary P. GILLIAM to Ms. A. E. STAINBACK: making colored silk dress (2.50), 2 yds. of cambrie (.30), 1 yd. silk facing (.75), 1 yd. of ribbon (.56), 2 hanks. of sewing silk (.13). [Paid] by Heller HILL? $4.24.

5. 1856, 22 May. R. H. GILLIAM, Grd. [Guardian], R. Gilliam. To Sarah E. MATHEWS: making 2 pr. pants (1.00), making 3 cot. shirts (1.13).

Tanning Hides

1. 1832, 3 Dec. Received of William S. CONER, 1 hide to tan. C. HARRIS.

2. 1856. Mrs. Mary WHITEHEAD, with E. P. EVANS: qr. train oil (.25), 1 side want up? (2.75), ditto (2.25), 1 qr. train oil (.25), 1 qr. vinager (.12), 1 hide 15 lobs (1.50), by 3 hides, 40 lob (4.80), 1 qr. vinager (.12). ... [plus other unknown items. One payment made by Edward J. GILLIAM].

Sawmills and Lumber

1. 1826, 25 Dec. Mr. Richard GILLIAM in acct. with John BONDURANT: To sawing 244 planks at 50 cent per hundred (1.22).

2. John D. GILLIAM, in acct. with Wm. J. SPENCER.
1845, 16 Feb.: sawing 415 feet plank (2.07).
1846: sawing 314 feet, plank (1.72), bought 24 feet scantling (.48), sawing 265 feet (1.32), sawing 218 feet (1.09).
1847: threshing crop wheat (1.25).

3. 1855, 1 Sep. R. H. GILLIAM, acct. to ANDERSON & LACKLAND: to 505 feet of 2 in plank (4.79), to 490 feet of flooring (6.85), to 1 lot of staves (2.50), to eugri? house (23.00).

4. 1858, 11 Feb. Col. Richard H. GILLIAM to Wm. J. SPENCER: to sawing 11 logs, 2697 feet, @ 3/ per hundred (134.48 1/2). Rec'd payment in full - Wm. J. SPENCER by Wm. G. SPENCER.

Medical and Dental Bills

1. 1835, 30 Dec. Mr. James BROWN in acct. with J. M. AUSTIN, Dr.: racking 2 teeth Negro SAM (2.00).

2. 1838. Major R. GILLIAM, administrator for Mr. HUNT, to P. H. ELCAN, Dr. [Patrick Henry ELCAN]: to visit and dressing insolent ulcer (15.00). Received in full of Mr. J. T. LIGON, 4 March 1840. P. H. ELCAN.

3. 1846. Mr. Littleberry HARDIMAN to Lydia GORDON: to visit as midwife to your two women, JINNY & BARBARA (4.00). Received in full of R. H. GILLIAM, admr. of L. B. HARDIMAN, dec., 28 Oct 1847.

4. 1849, 4 Feb. Mrs. GILLIAM [Mrs. R. H. GILLIAM] with Wm. M. SWOOPE: to visit & med[icine] for self at Col's plantation (3.00).

5. 1849, Jan 18 & 19. Mr. John GARY with Wm. M. SWOOPE, Dr.: to visit to self at Col. GILLIAM'S plantation, preparing powders? (3.00), quinine pills (.50).

6. Richard H. GILLIAM in a/c with Charles E. DAVIDSON, Dr.
1849, June: to attending Willie 5 days (5.00), services rendered BOB (10.00).

1850: to visit, medicine, attending WILSON, WILLIE, HENRY, AGIE, Tower Hill, a child, Mrs. GILLIAM, JANE, AMANDA; to corterising and quinine pills, Mrs. GILLIAM; cupping SUCKIE; bleeding JACK; cupping JACK; dressing wound B. BROWN; dressing wound, HARRY.
$50.00 [Total bill for 1849 and 1850]

7. 1853. Maj. R. H. GILLIAM to Wm. P. & A. MOSELEY, Dr.: to visit negro man (2.00), to visit wife, 4 gr. Mor., 3iv f.8. Rhub. (3.00). Rec. payment - Arthur MOSELEY.

8. Richd. H. GILLIAM to Chas. F. MOSELEY, Dr.
1857, Aug.: to visit boy at Institute (2.00), consultation with Dr. PHILLIPS (5.00), spending night (5.00).
1858: May and Nov: to visit negro child and med (4.50), powders (4.25), woman, AMANDA & med (2.50), woman, AMANDA & bottle Sol-Morphine (2.50). [Final payment received 12 Nov 1860 - Alex. MOSELEY for C. F. MOSELEY.]

9. 1857, Dec 24-25. Major R. H. GILLIAM to Arthur MOSELEY: To visit & attendance on wife in accouchment [delivery of baby] (12.00); 1 gum nipple shield (.25).

10. Col. R. H. GILLIAM to J. L. TWYMAN, Dr.
1861: to call to woman BETSY & med (1.25); med to woman SARAH; visit to girl CHARY, BALSER, son FLOYD, SLAZEY - and med (36.25).
1862: to visit 14 Jan - Negro boy with measles (2.50); 21 Jan - 2 Negro boys (3.00); 23-24 Jan = several Negroes and med (7.50); 27 Jan - boy EDWARD for J. J. GILLIAM (2.00); 30 Jan - boys ED. & JOHN & med (2.50); Feb 1, 2, 3, 7, 12 - attending sick Negroes (15.00). [These plus other medical expenses total - $94.75. This bill with interest was fully paid March 1863.]

Roads, Tolls

1. 1845, April. Buckingham County Court. John T. BOCOCK, one of the road Commissioners, in pursuance of an order made at the last court, on the motion of John MORRIS and Nathan H. THORNTON for leave to open a road through the lands of Isham GILLIAM, this day returned a report. - Whereupon it is ordered that Isham GILLIAM proprietor and Charles GIL-LIAM tenant of the lands through which the road is proposed to be conducted, be summoned to appear here on the first day of the next term to show cause of

any they can why the road may not be opened according to law. A copy teste, R. ELDRIDGE, C.

2. 1858, March 24. Col. R. GILLIAM. To toll gate No. 3. To toll for 4 waggons and self on horseback to and from Farmville. Recd. payment in full - R. A. BOOKER, T.G.

3. 1858. Richard H. GILLIAM, Moses A. SPENCER, Tandy HOLMAN, Edwin STEGER, Catharine M. PERKINS, Thomas F. PERKINS, John J. GILLIAM and Arthur MOSELEY. To the clerk of Buckingham County Court - 1858 May order appointing Viewers to view a way for a road from Pickshin to the Hardwickersville road 20 copy 20.
June order adding Viewers to this already appointed 20 copy 20. R. K. IRVING, C.R.C.

Hotel and Tavern Bills

1. 1824, 18 May. Richmond, VA. Mr. GILLIAM to S. D. CRENSHAW: to 1 days board, self and horse (1.50), meal self and horse (1.00), bar bill (.13).

2. 1839, 22 Feb. Richmond. Mr. GILLIAM to Columbian Hotel: to days board of self at 0/6 (10.00), to meal (.50). Rec. payment - S. S. LUBAN.

3. 1855, 4 May. Richmond. Mr. R. H. GILLIAM. To St. Charles Hotel, Richmond, board, washing, bar (10.99). Rec. payment - P. O. SIMS.

Subscriptions

1. 1849, 15 June. Rec'd. of Jno. B. GARY, $2.00 in a/c of his subscription to the Richmond Republican - R. P. COBB, D.P.M.

2. 1860, 24 Aug, Richmond, VA. Richard H. GILLIAM. To Central Presbyterian (subscription) from 1 Jan 1860 to 1 Jan 1861. ($2.50)

3. 1862, 24 Apr. Rec'd. of Rev. Mr. BOWMAN for R. H. GILLIAM five dollars for Presbyterian. - F. N. WALKER, Agt.

4. 1869. Col. R. H. GILLIAM to Garys Post Office: Daily Republican, 2 qrs. to 1st Jan 1870 (.60), Weekly Dispatch, 2 qrs. to 1st Jan 1870 (.10), postage on letters - 2 (.08), balance due on 1 letter (.01).

Mercantile

1. 1850, 12 Sep [paid on this date by R. H. GILLIAM]. Mr. David FERGUSON in acct. with Joel G. BROWN & Co.: 11 yds flannel (4.21); 1 pat vesting, 1 pr salt sellars (.63); 2 1/4 yds. casimere, 2 yds. domestic (1.29); 1 grop buttons, 1 slip thread (.31); 1 cot. handkerchiefs (.25); 24 sole leather @.22 (5.28); 1 3/4 yds blue pilot cloth (2.19); thread, 1 doz. buttons (.31); 1 1/2 yrds. Linsey (.45); sugar @ 6, sugar @ 10 (.73); 6 Laguyra Coffee, 1 flask & whiskey (.95); 21 spool cotton (.06); 1 coffee self (1.00).

2. 1853. Col. R. H. GILLIAM in account with Joel G. BROWN: acct. due $10.20; 8 yds calico (1.00); 1 vial anti:? wine (.10); 1 land slide (.75); 1 land bar (.25); 4 pr. lines (.40);4 lbs ad candles per self (1.50); 2 putty (.17); 1 yd. col. Cambree (.10); 1 bottle castor oil, pr. Wilson (.50); 1 box Peters Pills, self (.25); Cake Shaving soap (.19); 2 viles laudnam per order (.20); 1 bottle pain extracter (.25); 1 pad lock of boy (.88); 1 ditto self (.88); 2 lbs epsam salts (.25). Paid by W. LIPSCOMB $11.00. on 5 April 1853. Due 31 Aug 1853 $6.87.

PARTNERSHIP OF JOEL G. BROWN AND RICHARD H. GILLIAM

Articles of an agreement made and entered into this the 17th day of September 1849 between Joel G. Brown of the 1st part and Richard H. Gilliam of the second part witnesseth that the said Brown & Gilliam have this day agreed and entered into partnership under the firm and style of Joel G. Brown & Co., for the purpose of carrying on the mercantile business at Buckingham Court House for the term of three years from the 1st day of September 1849 on the following terms. It is understood and agreed between the parties, that each party, that is the said Brown & Gilliam shall pay into the concern within the time of ten months from the date of this contract Fifteen Hundred dollars each and the said Brown shall give the business his personal attention and for such service the said Brown shall receive from the concern two hundred dollars per annum and shall also charge the concern with one hundred dollars on account of his board and it is further understood and agreed between the parties that they shall keep a young man in the store and his board and wages shall be charged to the concern as may be agreed on and it is distinctly understood and agreed between the parties that they are equal partners and the net profits of the store are to be equally divided between them or their legal representatives and it is further agreed that neither partner shall use the name of the concern for any purpose except in such matters as may relate or concern the partnership.

Year	Buyer or Payee	Company	Type or Location
1825	Edward J. Gilliam	McKinney s & Clay	Pc Goods -(Glenmore)
1831	Edmund Glover	Wm. M. Evans	
1831	Wm. S. Conner	Wm. D Jones	Groc & Clothing-(New Store)
1835	Wm. S. Conner	Josiah Moseley CO	Shoes-Whiskey-Blk Powder
1834	W. Samuel Gregory	Frs. Thornton	Corn by barrel
1836	Col. R. H. Gilliam	R. G. Gary	Domestics & Gen Mdse.
1839	------?-----------	Gilliam Morning ? & Co.Spader	
1839	R. H. Gilliam	Moseley-Spencer Co.	Powder
1842	Mrs. Lucy C. Gary	J & E B Moseley Co	Gen Mdse.
1842	Thos. W. Isbell & Wm. Isbell	Flood & Trent Co	(Henry D & Thos Trent)
1840	Mrs. Lucy C. Gary	N. W. Jones	Domestics
1842	court suit	Branch & Holman	
1843	Samuel S. Sayne	Bryant & Young	Wilson P Bryant & Wm T Young
1842	Col. R. H. Gilliam	Flood & Nowlin	
1843	Lewis W. Cabell suit	Peters & Wells	
1843	court suit	Joseph Brightwell & Wm. C. Flourney	
1844	court suit	William H. Word & Quinn M. Word late merchants & Partners = Brightwell Co.	
1844	court suit	Hancock & Adams	
1843	Benj. S. Morris	Thomas S. & Charles A. Morton Co.	
1844	William W. Ferguson & Robert Rives	Partners in William W. Ferguson Co	
1847	John D. Gilliam	Scott & Davis	Gen .Mdse.
1849	Preston H. Spiller	Anderson D. Abraham	China
1849	John D. Gilliam	James Brown	En Mdse.
1851	R. H. Gilliam	Wm H. Word	Domestics
1851	Col. R. H. Gilliam	R G & J. B Gary	Groc & Gen. Mdse
1852	Wilson Garrett	W C Word	Domestics
1850	John B. Gary	Abraham & Moseley	Hardware * Domestics
1850	Richard H. Gilliam	George M Johnson	Brandy & Butter
1853	Mrs. Mary Whitehead	Wm S Wise	Gen Mdse.
1854	Richard H. Gilliam	P I Garret	Pocket Knife
1854	Col R. H. Gilliam	S A & J B Glover	Gen Mdse.
1853	Col R. H. Gilliam	Joel G Brown	Gen Mdse.
1857	Mrs. Mary Whithead	L D Jones	Clothing
1859	Col .R. H. Gilliam	Glover & Moseley	Gen Mdse.
1859	Richard H. Gilliam	Moseley & Garret	Pt Whiskey
1860	Col. R. H. Gilliam	Glover & Moseley	Pd account
1866	Col. R. H. Gilliam	J L Wert & Co	Domestics & Groc
1869	------?-----------	S B & J A Stegar	Gen Mdse.
1872	Col. R. H. Gilliam	Stegar , Garnett & Co	Gen Mdse.
1876	Col. R. H. Gilliam	Anderson & Morgan	Gen Mdse.

To all sheriffs, sergeants, mayors, bailiffs & constables in the
Commonwealth of Virginia.
Buckingham County to wit

Complaint being made to me, D. **Gurrant** a Justice of the peace for said
county upon oath by George W. **Kyle** deputy for George **Christian,**
Sheriff of Buckingham County that Alfred **Childers** was taken in custody
of the said sheriff by virtue of a capias ad respondendum in the name of
Russell M. **Smith** for the sum of Sixty Dollars did on or about the 22nd of
this month escape out of the custody of the said Sheriff and is now going at
large, these are therefore in the name of the commonwealth to require you
and every of you in your respective counties, cities, town, precincts to siege
and retake the said Alfred **Childers** and him so retaken to commit to the
prison where debtors are usually kept in the county where he is retaken and
deliver him to the Keeper there of together with this warrant hereby
commanding and requiring the said Keeper to receive the said Alfred
Childers and him safely keep in the said Jail without bail or mainprise until
satisfaction be made to the said Russell M. **Smith** for the said debt & cost
or until he be thence delivered by due course of law and to return this
warrant to the court of the county of Buckingham pursuant to the act of the
general assembly in that case made & provided. Given under my hand &
seal this the 26th day of October 1835

D. **Gurrant**

Buckingham C H, Sept 9, 1840
Received of Moseley, **Gilliam and Thornton,** in a settlement
this day, the sum of Nineteen Hundred & twenty dollars in full for the first
and second payments for my Sheriffalty leaving a balance due from them
Nine Hundred & sixty dollars to be paid at the expiration of my term of
office.

John **Morris**

Know all men by these presents that I Josiah **Moseley** of
Buckingham County having an interest in the Sheriffalty of Thomas
Pittman & James Meredith, Esqs, provided the said **Pittman and**
Meredith shall live to qualify as high sheriff of the county of Buckingham
in the years 1843 & 1845, I do hereby convey to Richard H. **Gilliam** of
Buckingham County all the interest which I have in & to the Sheriffalty
aforesaid for and during the term of the above mentioned, for and in
consideration of the sum of five hundred Dollars to me in hand paid by the
said Richard H. **Gilliam,** which said sum I bind myself to give bond &
security to refund to the said Gilliam in case of the death of the said **Pittman**
& **Meredith** before they shall be entitled to execute the duties of high
Sheriff of Buckingham, or in an equal proportion in case of the death of
either. Given under my hand this 7th day of Nov. 1842

Josiah **Moseley**

Received November 7, 1842 of Richard H. **Gilliam** five Hundred Dollars in full for my interest in the Sheriffally for the next four years.

Jos. **Moseley**

William M. **Moseley** has this day furnished me with fifty dollars on act of himself and **Richard H. Gilliam** to be used in attending to the interest of the Sheriffality of Buckingham, before the execution department at Richmond. Given under my hand this 24th day of June 1845.

J W Meredith

LETTER TO: Col. Richard H. **Gilliam**
              Buckingham C. H., Va.

FROM: J. H. **French**, Charleston, Sept 1846

Sir: I have to inform you that at our last court administration of the estate of the late Dr. **Meredith** was granted to his widow. I have also the satisfaction to inform you that from all I can learn is his estate is amply sufficient to pay all his debts. I have not as yet brought suit upon the bonds you placed in my hands, as judgment cannot now be had at our approaching term in October and there will be abundant time to obtain the judgment at the next spring term after hearing from you. I have therefore determined not to bring suit until I hear from you. I wish you to write me immediately and give me all the information that may be necessary in the prosecution of these suits. I wish you to furnish all the credits you are willing to allow with a precise account of the time you were in office and the abatement that is to be made by reason of the division of the county of Buckingham. [forming of Appomattox County, 1845]. There is no assignment on the note executed to Josiah **Moseley**, but as a memo, on the back of it states that the money for which it was executed was advanced by you. I imagine that suit on it must be brought for your benefit. Upon looking at the bonds and the contract by which you and William M. Mosely purchased the Sheriffalty, I find that they are all executed on the same day, 12th April 184__?. It may be necessary that I should be able to explain why the note executed to Josiah **Moseley** was not executed to you, since you advanced the money and since the contract for the Sheriffalty is made directly with you. The whole transaction having taken place on the same day I do not know that an explanation of this will be of any importance, but in the course of the trial it might be. If the Arbitration bond should be necessary I will let you know. Please answer immediately.

Respectfully yours,
J. H. **French**

To the Sheriff of Buckingham County

You are hereby ordered to keep in your custody the body of Wm W **Harvey** so that you have the body of the said **Harvey** before the next court for the county aforesaid to answer the charges named in the written warrant. Given under my hand this the 3rd November 1844.

E. J. **Gilliam**

APPRENTICESHIP OF RICHARD GILLIAM
TO COACH PAINTING AND TRIMMING

Memorandum of an agreement made and entered into this 13th day of July 1853, between Richard H. **Gilliam**, Guardian of Richard **Gilliam**, son of Jno. D. **Gilliam**, Dec., and Thomas H. **Merryman** both of the County of Buckingham, Va., witnesseth that the said Richard H. **Gilliam**, Gar., has put the boy above named with the said Thomas H. **Merryman** to learn and be instructed in the trade and art of Coach Painting, and Trimming and it is agreed between the parties that the said boy shall remain with the said Merryman for the term of three years and five months from the date of this article and the said Merryman binds himself to instruct the said boy in all the arts of said trade and to keep him employed on work of that sort and give him a thorough knowledge of Coach painting and trimming and the said Merryman agrees to clothe, board and take care of the said boy during the said term in a comfortable and wholesome manner and necessary attention paid and expenses during any illness or sickness that may befall him and it is also agreed between the parties that the said boy Richard **Gilliam** shall have at least ten months schooling during the term of service say three years and five months, in a good school with teacher competent to instruct him to read and write and also to instruct him in arithmetic at least to the rule of three, and at the expiration of the term of service the said Merryman binds himself to give the said boy a good and neat suit of Sunday clothes. The treatment of the said boy at all times to be of a kind & parental character. Given under our hands and Seals this the day & date first above mentioned.

Thomas H. **Merryman** (Seal)

Abstract of the Will of Richard Gilliam
of Buckingham County, Virginia.

Record Book 12, p. 195-198, recorded July 19 1842, Rutherford Co., Tenn.

To: His wife: Elizabeth Gilliam, to have use and benefit of my plantation during her widowhood, and during this time the use and benefit of the following Negroes, viz. Harry and his wife Hannah, Mat, Danl., (1 yellow) Seth, Aggy, Nancy, a girl Rhoda, two boys Isaac and Powell, with their increases.

Also my will that she should take as much of my stock, plantation tools, household and kitchen furniture as may be necessary for her support during her widowhood, together with a sufficiency of provisions for the support of the plantation one year. At her death or marriage it is my will and desire that all of the above named negroes with their increases, together with my lands and all the stock, household and kitchen furniture, tools and crop that may be on hand at the time be sold by my Cos. [commissioners], and the proceeds arising therefrom equally divided among my children and their heirs or representatives as have herein after directed.

It is my will and desire at my death that the remaining part of my stock, crop, plantation tools, household and kitchen furniture that may be on hand after my aforesaid wife Elizabeth Gilliam shall have taken so much thereof as may be thought necessary for her support and use be sold and the proceeds thereof equally divided among my children their heirs or representatives as hereafter directed.

It is my will and desire that my tract of land lying on the head of Holiday Creek in Buckingham County, be sold by my executors whenever they may think best and the proceeds thereof equally divided among my children and their representatives as herein after directed.

I give to my son Edward J. Gilliam, the following negroes, viz. Mike, Rachel, Harrison and Stephen and to his heirs forever, also two beds and furniture which property I have valued to him at Nine Hundred and Seventeen Dollars.

I give to my son Glover D. Gilliam, the following negroes, viz. Stephen (son of Geo), James, which together with stock and furniture and money herefore furnished him, I have valued at Eleven Hundred and Ninety Dollars to him and his heirs for ever.

I give to my daughter Lucy C. Gary, the following negroes, viz. Sam, Charlie and Rozana, which together with stock and furniture furnished heretofore to her, I have valued to be at Nine Hundred and Sixty Dollars.

I give to my sons Edward J. Gilliam and Richard H. Gilliam in trust for the benefit of my daughter Sally W. Neighbours, and her heirs the following negroes, viz. Celia, Sophia, Mahala and Joe, which together with stock and furniture heretofore furnished her I have valued to her at Nine Hundred and Fifty Dollars.

I give to my son Richard H. Gilliam the following slaves, viz. Jack Judy, Delaware and Martha, also two beds and furniture which I have valued at Eight Hundred and Seventy Dollars.

I give to sons Edward J. Gilliam and Richard H. Gilliam in trust for the benefit of my daughter Eliza G. Gilliam and her heirs the following negroes, viz. Monroe, Louisia and Lucy, also bed and furniture I have valued to be at Nine Hundred and Thirty Dollars. The above negroes and their increase to be held for the benefit of my said daughter Eliza G. Gilliam, in trust of my said sons Edward J. Gilliam and Richard H. Gilliam.

It is also my will and desire that my daughter Eliza G. Gilliam, should live with her mother during her life if she my daughter Elizabeth should remain single so long free of charge.

I do hereby appoint my sons Edward J. Gilliam and Richard H. Gilliam my executors to this my last will and testament. This the Ninth day of February Eighteen Hundred and Thirty Three.

Witness: Richard Gilliam
William Gilliam
John H. Rowton
James Anderson

At a court held for Buckingham County this 9 day of Sept 1839. This will proved in open court and proved the oaths of William Gilliam and John H. Rowton.

And another court held on Monday the 9 day of December 1840, Edward J. Gilliam, one of the executors named took the oath of any Executor and together with Thomas Sanders and Thomas Gary his securities entered into and acknowledged a bond in the penalty of Forty Thousand Dollars, certificate granted him for obtaining a probate of the said will in due form.

Teste- Rolfe Eldridge, C.B.C.

Gilliam Family – The First Six Generations

William Gilliam m. Elizabeth --- (dau. of Epaphroditus Lawson, Isle of Wight)

Richard Gilliam m. Margaret Lawson

Epaphroditus Gilliam (New Kent Co., Va) m.------?

Epaphroditus Gilliam (b. 1727, d. 13 Sept 1789)* m. Elizabeth Holland, (d. 21 June 1799)

Richard Gilliam (b. 4 Apr 1760, d. 2 Aug 1839) m. 8 Mar 1798 Elizabeth A.Glover
(b. 3 May 1775-7, d. 13 Mar 1850), dau. of Edmund Glover

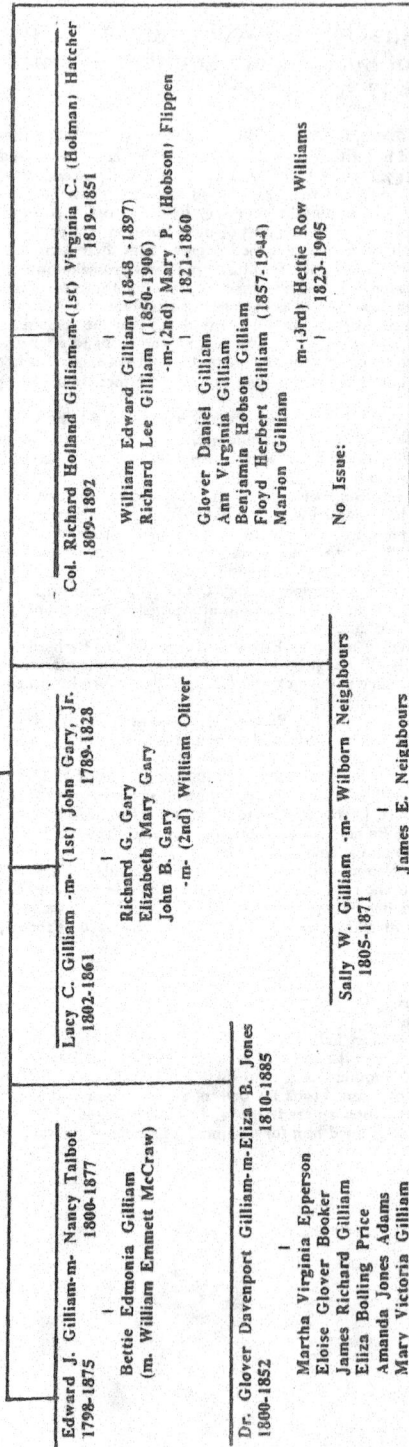

Edward J. Gilliam-m- Nancy Talbot
1798-1875   1800-1877

  Bettie Edmonia Gilliam
  (m. William Emmett McCraw)

Dr. Glover Davenport Gilliam-m-Eliza B. Jones
1800-1852   1810-1885

  Martha Virginia Epperson
  Eloise Glover Booker
  James Richard Gilliam
  Eliza Bolling Price
  Amanda Jones Adams
  Mary Victoria Gilliam
  Edward Glover Gilliam
  Mary Marshall Gilliam
  Olivia Ford Wooding
  Walter Flood Gilliam
  Emma Josephine m (1st) Gilbert
            (2nd) Gooch

  Thomas West Gilliam

Lucy C. Gilliam -m- (1st) John Gary, Jr.
1802-1861   1789-1828

  Richard G. Gary
  Elizabeth Mary Gary
  John B. Gary
  -m- (2nd) William Oliver

Sally W. Gilliam -m- Wilborn Neighbours
1805-1871

  James E. Neighbours

Col. Richard Holland Gilliam-m-(1st) Virginia C. (Holman) Hatcher
1809-1892   1819-1851

  William Edward Gilliam (1848 -1897)
  Richard Lee Gilliam (1850-1906)
    -m-(2nd) Mary P. (Hobson) Flippen
        1821-1860

  Glover Daniel Gilliam
  Ann Virginia Gilliam
  Benjamin Hobson Gilliam (1857-1944)
  Floyd Herbert Gilliam (1857-1905)
  Marion Gilliam

    m-(3rd) Hettie Row Williams
        1823-1905

No Issue:

Elizabeth Glover Gilliam -m- (1st) William Gilliam
1812-1853

  Issue:
  Virginia Elizabeth Gilliam
    b. 22 Nov 1839
    d. 9 June 1847

  -m- (2nd) Richard Lawrence Anderson
    b. 22 May 1808 Cumberland, Co Va.
    d. 9 March 1870 Vera. Va.
    Issue:
  Edward Lawrence Anderson
    (1851-2-1903)

*Epaphroditus Gilliam was taxed on 375 acres in Buckingham County Va in 1782.

COLONEL RICHARD HOLLAND GILLIAM
(1809 - 1892)

and the Gilliam Family

Born on 1 April 1809 in Buckingham County, Virginia, he was the son of Richard Gilliam (1760-1839) and Elizabeth Glover Gilliam (1777-1850). His grandparents on the Gilliam side were Epaphroditus Gilliam II (1727-1789) and Elizabeth Holland Gilliam (died 1799). [For earlier generations of the Gilliam lineage see previous page.]

Throughout most of his life he was addressed as Captain, Major or Colonel in recognition of his role in the Virginia Militia of Buckingham County. For the years 1832-1842 he served on the militia court martial for the First and Second Battalions of the 24th Regiment, Virginia Militia. They met at Spreading Oak, Curdsville, William Newton's and Fountain's Mill, in Buckingham County.

On 25 August 1831, at age 22, he joined Maysville Presbyterian Church (Buckingham Court House), just seven years after the church was established. He was listed as active Elder in 1834, 1843 and 1860. His first wife is buried in the churchyard.

Richard Holland Gilliam was married three times. He married first on 16 September 1847, Virginia Catherine Hatcher (1819-1851) widow of Joseph Hatcher and daughter of William and Jane (Ayres) Holman. He married second on 15 December 1852, Mary Page (Hobson) Flippen (1821-1860). She was the widow of Thomas D. Flippen and the daughter of Benjamin and Sally W. (Hatcher) Hobson. He married his third wife, Hettie Row Williams [1823-1905] on 28 April 1863. According to Miss Elsie W. Gilliam, they had been childhood sweethearts.[1]

Richard H. Gilliam owned a large plantation. In 1849 he paid taxes on 19 slaves and 11 horses. He was listed in the census of 1850 as hotel keeper; we believe that he operated the Maysville Hotel. He was a half partner in the Joel G. Brown & Co., a general store operating at Buckingham Court House. [See page 65 for the partnership agreement.] The 1860 census listed him as a farmer with a personal estate valued at $36,210 and real estate worth $10,000. He paid taxes on 2418 acres of land in 1880.

He was, for many years, active as Deputy Sheriff, serving Buckingham sheriffs, Thomas Pittman, R. B. Patteson and James P. Meredith during the 1840s. He also served as one of the commissioners for a new clerks office and courthouse after the fire of 1869. There were many other community boards on which he served: School Commission, Road Commission, Poor House Overseers. Over a period of years he opposed the formation of the new county of Appomattox.

In the following sections are given the descendants of Richard Holland Gilliam and some of those of his brothers and sisters. The paragraph number [followed by a period] is a key to tracking a lineage. Note for instance, the number 12 below is given preceding the name of Bettie Edmonia Gilliam. This indicates that a paragraph number 12 follows which contains more information on Bettie Edmonia Gilliam and her descendants. The paragraph numbers are in numerical order. The number appearing in brackets is the generation number, the first generation being that of William Gilliam, the first shown on the chart on the page 66. We continue here with the sixth through tenth generations.

SIXTH GENERATION

6. Edward J.[6] Gilliam (Richard, 5). Born, 13 Dec 1798. Died, 25 Mar 1875. He married Nancy Talbott, 23 Mar 1848.[2] Born, circa 1800.[3] Died, 29 Mar 1877. Edward J. Gilliam was the original owner of Millcote. Child:
   12   i. Bettie Edmonia[7] Gilliam.

7. Glover Davenport[6] Gilliam (Richard, 5). Born, 25 Aug 1800. Died, 22 Sep 1852. Burial in the home place, "Landover, " Campbell Co., VA. He entered Hampden-Sidney College in 1818. In 1824 he graduated with honors from Medical College of Philadelphia. For a while he conducted his medical practice at New Store, Buckingham Co. In 1826 he moved to Campbell Co. and purchased the farm of Major Rudd, located on Falling River, seven miles from Brookneal. The home was named "Landover," since Dr. Gilliam also owned a tract of land on the other side of the river. Here Dr. Gilliam practiced medicine and operated a plantation of about 1800 acres including a mill on Falling River. He married Eliza Bolling Jones (1810-1885). She was a descendant of Pocahontas and John Rolfe. Their children:
   13   i. Martha Virginia[7] Gilliam.
   14   ii. Eloise Glover Gilliam.
   15   iii. James Richard Gilliam.

16   iv. Eliza Bolling Gilliam.
       v. Amanda Jones Gilliam. Born, 27 Nov 1836. Died, 22 Feb 1920.[4]
She married Richard E. Adams.
      vi. Mary Victoria Gilliam. Born, 4 Jul 1838. Died, 10 May 1840.
17   vii. Edward Glover Gilliam.
     viii. Mary Marshall Gilliam. Born, 26 Jul 1842. Died, 1854.
18   ix. Olivia Ford Gilliam.
19   x. Walter Flood Gilliam.
20   xi. Emma Josephine Gilliam.
21   xii. Thomas West Gilliam.

8.   Lucy C.[6] Gilliam (Richard, 5). Born, 29 Dec 1802. Died, 31 Mar 1861.
She married, first, John Gary, Jr., son of John Gary and Mary Bush, 17 Oct
1822. Born, 9 Jun 1789. Died, 21 Jan 1828. Children:
       i. Richard G.[7] Gary. Born, 26 May 1824.
      ii. Elizabeth Mary Gary. Born, 3 May 1826. Married Preston Henry
Spiller 22 Nov 1843.
      iii. John B. Gary. Born, 2 Jan 1828.

She married, second, William Oliver, 6 Mar 1850. Born, circa 1793.

9.   Sally W.[6] Gilliam (Richard, 5). Born, 15 Dec 1805. Died, 24 Jun 1871.
She married Wilborn Neighbours. Born, circa 1806.[5] Children:
       i. James E.[7] Neighbours. Born, circa 1829.[6]

10. Richard Holland[6] Gilliam (Richard, 5). Born, 1 Apr 1809. Died, 16
Jan 1892. Burial in Spring Hill Cemetery, Lynchburg, VA. He married, first,
Virginia C. Holman, daughter of William Holman and Jane Ayres, 16 Sep
1847. Born, 12 Sep 1819. Died, 21 Nov 1851. Burial in Maysville Pres.,
Church, Buckingham C.H., VA. Children:
22   i. William Edward[7] Gilliam.
23   ii. Richard Lee Gilliam. Both William Edward and Richard Lee
were baptized on 13 Jul 1851; and both joined 16 Oct 1864 the Presbyterian
Church, Buckingham C.H., VA. Richard Lee moved to Maysville, AL at an
early age.

He married, second, Mary Page Hobson Flippen, daughter of Benjamin
Hobson and Sally W. Hatcher, 15 Dec 1852 in Powhatan Co., VA. Born, 14
May 1821. Died, 22 Sep 1860. Children:
      iii. Glover Daniel Gilliam. Born, 22 Oct 1853. Died, 3 Dec 1855.
      iv. Ann Virginia Gilliam. Born, 19 Apr 1855. Died, 29 Jul 1855.

v. Benjamin Hobson Gilliam. Born, 10 Jul 1856. Died, 1 Oct 1857.
24   vi. Floyd Herbert Gilliam.
vii. Marion Gilliam. Born, 22 Apr 1859. Died, 10 Aug 1859.

He married, third, Hettie Row Williams, daughter of Jehu Williams and Hettie, 28 Apr 1863. Born, 7 Feb 1823. Died, 30 Oct 1905. Burial in Spring Hill Cemetery, Lynchburg, VA. They had no children.

11.   Elizabeth Glover[6] Gilliam (Richard, 5). Born, 17 Feb 1812. Died, 7 May 1853. She married, first, William Gilliam. He died 2 March 1842 in Rutherford Co., TN. Child:
i. Virginia Elizabeth Gilliam. Born 22 Nov 1839. Died, 9 Jun 1847.

She married, second, Richard Lawrence Anderson (1808-1870), 18 Nov 1848 or 1849. Children:
ii. Edward Lawrence Anderson. Born 20 Jan 1851-2. Died 10 Apr 1903, buried family plot, Vera, VA. Married Codelia Lewis, daughter of Shadreck and Virginia Lewis, 20 Sept 1879. Their children: Eliza Ann Anderson, Edgar Anderson, Richard Alexander Anderson, Dabney William Anderson.

SEVENTH GENERATION

12.   Bettie Edmonia[7] Gilliam (Edward J., 6). Born, circa 1848.[7] Died, 1922. She married William Emmett McCraw. Born, 20 Apr 1846, in The Pines. Died, 22 May 1920. Children:
i. Richard Miller[8] McCraw. Born, 29 Sep 1868. Died, 18 Nov 1931. He married Elizabeth Bowcock Watts, 7 Jul 1926.
ii. Mary Emma McCraw. Born, 5 Apr 1871. Died, 10 Sep 1910.[8] She married Charles Dancy McCraw, 20 Jun 1887.[9]
iii. Edward Cary McCraw. Born, 5 Jun 1873. Died, 31 Aug 1953. He married Emma Walton Keller, 30 Dec 1903.
iv. Lucy Lee McCraw. Born, 20 Jun 1885. Died, 8 Aug 1956. She married Nathaniel White Kuykendall, 19 May 1909.

13.   Martha Virginia[7] Gilliam (Glover Davenport, 6). Born, 7 Jan 1830. She married Joseph Epperson. Children:
i. Glover Egbert[8] Epperson.

14.   Eloise Glover[7] Gilliam (Glover Davenport, 6). Born, 22 Mar 1832. Died, 24 Feb 1870. She married Richard Edward Booker. He was a Baptist Pastor at Naruna, VA. Children:
i. Sallie Love[8] Booker. She married H. T. Booker.

    ii. Richard Glover Booker.
   iii. Walter T. Booker. He married Fannie Foster.
   iv. Norman Courtney Booker. He married Lillian Bell.
    v. Loulie Emma Booker. She married Jesse T. Adams.
   vi. George Richard Booker. Died young.

15.   James Richard[7] Gilliam (Glover Davenport, 6). Born, 3 Oct 1833. Died, 1855. He married Annie Slaughter Davenport. Children:
    i. James Richard[8] Gilliam. Born, 1854. Died, 1917. He married Jessie Belfield Johnson.

16.   Eliza Bolling[7] Gilliam (Glover Davenport, 6). Born, 20 May 1835. Died, 19 Jan 1894. She married Richard Price. Occupation: Doctor. Children:
    i. Infant[8]. Died in enroute to Tennessee at Hollins.
       Burial in Enon Baptist Church Cemetery.
   ii. Eliza Bolling Price. She married --- Melton.
   iii. Daisy Price. She married --- Broyler.
   iv. Motie Price. She married Morton Price.
    v. William Jones Price.
   vi. Thomas West Price.
   vii. Nathaniel Price.

17.   Edward Glover[7] Gilliam (Glover Davenport, 6). Born, 9 Mar 1840. Died, 9 Dec 1891. He married, first, Emma Plunkett Gilbert, 1869. Children:
    i. Ella Coleman[8] Gilliam. Born, 26 Nov 1870. Died, May 1945. She married C. Edward Evans.
   ii. John Richard Gilliam. Born, May 1871. Died, 1876.
   iii. Annie Eliza Gilliam. Born, 24 Mar 1872. She married Augustus H. Evans.
   iv. James Cornelius Gilliam. Born, 15 Jun 1874. He married Minnie Calaham, 1899.
    v. Walter Edward Gilliam. Born, 14 Oct 1878. Died, Jun 1941.
   vi. Fannie Jane Gilliam. Born, 14 Mar 1880. She married William C. Cook, 1909.
   vii. Emma Hubbard Gilliam. Born, 31 Jul 1881. She married Daniel P. Mix, 1900.

He married, second, Colie Tynes, 1882.

18.   Olivia Ford[7] Gilliam (Glover Davenport, 6). Born, 11 Apr 1844. Died, 4 Feb 1907. She married Thomas H. Wooding. Children:
    i.   Martha Susan[8] Wooding. Married Leigh Budwell.
    ii.   Eliza Gilliam Wooding. She married Silas Carter.
    iii.   Loulie M. Berger Wooding.
    iv.   Ella Wilcox Wooding. She married Thomas Carter.
    v.   Robert H. Wooding. He married, first, Virginia Eamons. He married, second, Elizabeth Carter.
    vi.   Alice Wooding m. Silas Carter.
    vii.   Emma Wooding. She married John Shapard.
    viii.   Willie Hill Wooding.
    ix.   Thomas W. Wooding. He married Ethel Booker.
    x.   Samuel Josiah Wooding.
    xi.   Lillian Wooding. She married, first, Winston. She married, second, J. W. Kent.
    xii.   James Richard Wooding. He married Jane Smith.
    xiii.   West Gilliam Wooding. He married Bessie Moses.
    xiv.   Nathaniel Wooding. He married Ola Reynolds.

19.   Walter Flood[7] Gilliam (Glover Davenport, 6). Born, 27 Jan 1846. Died, 3 Feb 1926. He married Jane Lewis Hamlet, 30 Jan 1866. Died, 1916. Children:
    i.   Armistead Hamlet[8] Gilliam. He married Mrs. Anna Steel Ramsey.
    ii.   Eliza Bolling Gilliam. She married Martin Whitlow.
    iii.   Sallie Virginia Gilliam. Died, 1959. Never married.
    iv.   Olivia West Gilliam. She married William Jones Abbitt.
    v.   Robert Edward Gilliam. Married Annie Holmes Henry.
    vi.   Walter Fuqua Gilliam. Died 1964. Never married.
    vii.   Glover Davenport Gilliam. Married Russie Turner.
    viii.   James Thomas Gilliam.Married Sallie Bowman.
    ix.   Rosa Maria Gilliam.
    x.   Ruth Jane Gilliam. Both Rosa and Ruth Jane were living at "Landover, in 1964. Neither married.

20.   Emma Josephine[7] Gilliam (Glover Davenport, 6). Born, 30 Apr 1848. Died, 1886. She married, first, George Gilbert, Nov 1865. Children:
    i.   Rosa Lee[8] Gilbert. She married J. B. Woodson.
    ii.   George W. Gilbert. He married Blanche Robertson.
    iii.   Cornelius Gilbert. He married Eva Sanderson.

iv. Annie Gilbert. She married W. A. Ford. Emma Josephine (Gilliam) Gilbert married, second, Charles Gooch. Children: John Gooch. and Emma Josephine Gooch who married Floyd Knight.

21. Thomas West[7] Gilliam (Glover Davenport, 6). Born, 21 Nov 1849. Died, 2 Feb 1924. He married Fannie Diuguid. Children:
    i. Elsie West[8] Gilliam.
    ii. Grace Schenk Gilliam. She married Edward F. Younger of Brookneal, VA. 1907.
    iii. Fannie Diuguid Gilliam.

22. William Edward[7] Gilliam (Richard Holland, 6). Born, 20 Jul 1848. Died, 18 May 1897. Buried at Millcote, Buckingham Co. He married Margaret Daniel Mathews, daughter of William Daniel Mathews and Margaret Gilliam, 30 Jan 1878.[10] Born, 21 Aug 1855. Died, 22 Apr 1926. Burial in Hollywood Cemetery, Richmond, VA. Children:
  25 i. Margaret Virginia[8] Gilliam.
    ii. William Lee Gilliam. Born, 19 Apr 1880. Died, 2 Apr 1950. Married Annie Franklin Barnes. Their son William Lee, Jr. born 1 July 1917.
    iii. Marshall Robertson Gilliam. Born, 26 Oct 1881. Died 6 April 1964. Married Anne Bootwright b. 6 Jan 1890, d. 28 Apr 1959.
  26 iv. Edward Holland Gilliam.
    v. Frank Daniel Gilliam. Born, 17 Apr 1885. Died, 27 Jan 1903.
  27 vi. Henry Eugene Gilliam.
    vii. Marion Williams Gilliam. Born, 3 Apr 1890. Died, 7 Jan 1963. He married Mary Barber Tice. Their children:
      (1) David Gilliam married Patricia Hollis. Their issue: Patricia Diane and David Michael.
      (2) Margaret (Peggy) Gilliam married John P. Tice. Their issue: John P. Jr., Pamela E. and James R.
      (3) Robert (Bobby) Gilliam married Dora Chadwick. Their issue: Robert L., Thomas A., Matthew Holman and Marion W.
      (4) Marion Gilliam married Carol Batten. Their issue: Stephen, Terrence, Paul and John.

23. Richard Lee[7] Gilliam (Richard Holland, 6). Born, 13 Jul 1850, in Buckingham Co., VA. Died, 6 Jan 1906, in Huntsville, AL. Burial in Maple Hill Cemetery, Huntsville, AL. He married Mary (Mollie) Lawler, daughter of William Lawler and Martha Byrne, 12 Dec 1876, in Huntsville, AL. Born, 7 Nov 1855, in Maysville, AL. Died, 6 Apr 1944, in Chattanooga, TN. Burial

in Maple Hill Cem., Huntsville, AL. Children:

    i. Richard Holland[8] Gilliam. Born, 17 Jul 1878, in Maysville, AL. Died, 14 Jul 1899, in Maysville, AL. Burial in Byrne Cemetery Maysville, AL. Never married.

    ii. William Ernest Gilliam. Born, 24 Dec 1880, in Maysville, AL. Died, 2 Feb 1894, in Maysville, AL. Burial in Byrne Cemetery, Maysville, AL.

    28 iii. Georgia Williams Gilliam.

    iv. Mattie Lee Gilliam. Born, 7 Mar 1886, in Maysville, AL. Died, 18 Aug 1963, in Chattanooga, TN.

    v. Robert Lawler Gilliam. Born, 18 May 1891, in Maysville, AL. Died, 22 Apr 1961, in Chattanooga, TN. He married Mae Simmons, 4 Jul 1924, in Chattanooga, TN. No issue.

24. Floyd Herbert[7] Gilliam (Richard Holland, 6). Born, 24 Dec 1857, in Buckingham, Co., VA. Died, 8 Jun 1944, in Huntsville, AL. Christened, 28 Sep 1860, in Presbyterian Church, Buckingham C.H. Moved to Maysville, Alabama as a young man. He married Bobbie Lee Lawler, daughter of William Jesse Lawler and Octavia Byrne, 22 Nov 1882, in Maysville, AL. Born, 27 Dec 1864, in Maysville, AL. Died, 11 Jul 1940, in Huntsville, AL. Both buried at Maple Hill Cemetery Huntsville, AL. Children:

    i. Mary Jessie[8] Gilliam. Born, 25 Jan 1884, in Maysville, AL. Died, 19 Dec 1961, in Huntsville, AL. Burial in Maple Hill Cemetery. She married William Calvin Davis, 29 Dec 1909, in Huntsville, AL. No children.

    ii. Infant son Gilliam. Born, 12 Feb 1887, in Maysville, AL. Died, 17 Feb 1887, in Maysville, AL. Burial in Lawler Cemetery, Maysville, AL

    iii. William Herbert Gilliam. Born, 24 Jul 1888, in Maysville, AL. Died, 21 Jan 1961, in Chattanooga, TN. Burial in Maple Hill, Huntsville, AL. He married Elva Holmes, 17 Sep 1921, in Huntsville, AL. No children.

    29 iv. John Floyd Gilliam.

    30 v. Richard Holland Gilliam.

EIGHTH GENERATION

25. Margaret Virginia[8] Gilliam (William Edward, 7). Born, 25 Dec 1878. Died, 15 Jun 1942. She married George Hannah Elcan, son of Marcus C. Elcan and Laura Adelaide Hannah, 27 Dec 1906. Born, 28 Apr 1876. Died, 21 Sep 1965. They built and lived at "Elk Hearst," Buckingham Co., VA. (Most of the Elcan family are buried in the family plot at "Elk Hall," plantation. Their children:

31 i. William Cleveland[9] Elcan. Born, 28 Jan 1908. Died, 18 Jan 1985.
    ii. Henry Eugene Elcan. Born, 23 Oct 1911. Died, 3 Jan 1985, in
Dillwyn, VA m. July 19, 1929, Opal Lucille Dial, b. 2 Dec, 1907.
32 iii. George Hannah Elcan, Jr.
    iv. Margaret Adelaide Elcan. Born, 5 Jun 1916. She married, first,
George Hamilton Lacy (died 6 Jun 1955) and she married, second, William Coleman Taylor (died 4 Jun 1985).
33 v. Virginia Estelle Elcan.

26. Edward Holland[8] Gilliam (William Edward, 7). Born, 28 Jun 1883.
Died, 9 Oct 1936. He married Lucy Irving Elcan, 26 Nov 1913. Born, 22
Feb 1889. Children:
    i. Margaret[9] Hannah Gilliam. She married first, T. D. Payne and
second, Howard Strock.
27. Henry Eugene[8] Gilliam (William Edward, 7). Born, 17 Apr 1888.
Died, 12 Aug 1953. He married Juliet Jefferson Hundley (10 Nov 1886 -
10 Jul 1970). Child:
    i. Lucy Waller[9] Gilliam. Born 9 Jan 1926. She married Edwin J.
Crockin. Born 9 Feb 1916. Died 18 Jul 1984.

28. Georgia Williams[8] Gilliam (Richard Lee, 7). Born, 25 May 1882, in
Maysville, AL. Died, 20 Aug 1968, in Chattanooga, TN. She married
James William Donaldson, 12 Oct 1910, in Huntsville, AL. Died, 19 Dec
1945, in Chattanooga, TN. Children:
34 i. Dorothy Louise[9] Donaldson.
35 ii. Edith Gray Donaldson.
36 iii. Robert Walter Donaldson.

29. John Floyd[8] Gilliam (Floyd Herbert, 7). Born, 20 Nov 1894, in
Maysville, AL. Died, 14 Jan 1982, in Huntsville, AL. Burial in Maple Hill
Cemetery. He married Bessie Graham, 1 Jul 1916. Children:
37 i. Dorothy Graham[9] Gilliam.
    ii. Jane Gilliam. Born, 16 Nov 1919, in Huntsville, AL. Died, 24 Apr
1920, in Huntsville, AL. Burial in Maple Hill Cemetery.
38 iii. John Robert Gilliam.

30. Richard Holland[8] Gilliam (Floyd Herbert, 7). Born, 7 Oct 1897, in
Maysville, AL. Died, 24 Jan 1976, in Huntsville, AL. Burial in Maple Hill
Cemetery. He married Mayme Allen Blackwell, 8 Sep 1924, in
Huntsville, AL.

Children:
39   i. Richard Holland[9] Gilliam, Jr.
40   ii. Thomas Allen Gilliam.

NINTH GENERATION

31. William Cleveland[9] Elcan. Born, 28 Jan 1908. Died, 18 Jan 1985. He married Ruth Winstone Edmonds. Children:
    i. Ruth Virginia[10] Elcan (Pelham, Mass.).

32. George Hannah[9] Elcan. Born, 13 Oct 1913. Died, 10 Dec 1954. He married Anna Meade Burnett, daughter of Eddie Samuel Burnett and Iturea Elizabeth Weeks, 4 Dec 1948, in Floyd, VA. Born, 19 Aug 1918, in Willis, Floyd Co., VA. Anna lives in Lynchburg, VA. Their children:
41   i. Anne[10] Burnett Elcan.
42   ii. George Hannah Elcan, III.

33. Virginia Estelle[9] Elcan. Born, 3 Mar 1924. She married Carl Coleman Rosen, 13 Sep 1946, in Lynchburg, VA. Born, 1 Mar 1920, in Lone Oak, Buckingham Co., VA. Children:
43   i. Margaret Lee[10] Rosen.
44   ii. Carl Coleman Rosen, Jr.

34. Dorothy Louise[9] Donaldson. Born, 29 Sep 1911, in Toga, VA. Died, 26 May 1990, in Atlanta, GA. She married Eugene Wilford Preble, 22 Feb 1941, in Chattanooga, TN. Child:
    i. Helen Elizabeth[10] Preble. Born, 15 Nov 1943, in Alexandria, VA. She married Alan Crawford Stewart, 23 Mar 1968, in Dallas, TX.

35. Edith Gary[9] Donaldson. Born, 4 Sep 1917, in Chattanooga, TN. Died, 14 Apr 1977, in Chattanooga, TN. She married Judge Russell Campbell Carden, 29 Mar 1941, in Albany, NY. Child:
45   i. Gary Russell [10] Carden.

36. Robert Walter[9] Donaldson. Born, 20 Mar 1920, in Chattanooga, TN. He married Mary Elizabeth Virgin, 17 Sep 1948, in Chattanooga, TN. Child:

46   i. Gary Ann[10] Donaldson.

37. Dorothy Graham[9] Gilliam (John Floyd, 8). Born, 9 Aug 1918, in Huntsville, AL. She married Richard Millard Fillmore, 12 Apr 1947, in Panama Canal Zone. Children:
    i. Richard Millard[10] Fillmore, Jr. Born, 4 Sep 1948, in Panama Canal Zone.

ii. John Rollin Fillmore. Born, 5 Apr 1952, in Puerto Rico.

38. John Robert[9] Gilliam (John Floyd, 8). Born, 7 Jul 1924, in Huntsville, AL. He married, first, Mary Willie Garvin, 28 Aug 1948, in Phenix City, AL. Died, 10 Oct 1973. Children:

    i. Sandra Wall[10] Gilliam. Born, 17 May 1949, in Auburn, AL. She married James Elton Jolley, 25 Jun 1979, in San Antonio, TX. They live in Texas.

47 ii. Mary Robyn Gilliam.

He married, second, Woodie Rae Robinson, 16 Sep 1978, in San Antonio, TX. The live at 115 Lake Placid Driver, Seguin, TX. No children.

39. Richard Holland[9] Gilliam, Jr. (Richard Holland, 8). Born, 24 Aug 1926, in Huntsville, AL. He married Catherine Russell Kelly, 19 Aug 1949, in Huntsville, AL. They live at 1708 Red Oak Road, Huntsville, AL. Children:

    i. Richard Holland[10] Gilliam, III. Born, 30 Nov 1950, in Huntsville, AL.

48 ii. Karen Kelly Gilliam.

    iii. David Allen Gilliam. Born, 9 Oct 1966, in Huntsville, AL.

40. Thomas Allen[9] Gilliam (Richard Holland, 8). Born, 25 Nov 1929, in Huntsville, AL. He married Ruth Kathrine Enzweiler, 16 Aug 1961, in Huntsville, AL. Children:

    i. Kristen Leigh[10] Gilliam. Born, 29 Jul 1962, in Huntsville, AL. She married Robert Nathan Tidmore, 4 Apr 1992, in Huntsville, AL.

    ii. Thomas Allen Gilliam, Jr. Born, 15 Nov 1963, in Huntsville, AL.

    iii. Mark Robert Gilliam. Born, 29 Nov 1968, in Huntsville, AL. He married Sharry Lynn (Weber) Neal, 29 Aug 1992, in Huntsvillle, AL

TENTH GENERATION

41. Anne[10] Elcan (George Hannah, 9). Born, 31 Mar 1950, in Southside Hospital, Farmville, VA. She married David Cyrus Judd. Born 6 Sep 1949. Children:

    i. Elizabeth Burnett[11] Judd. Born, 21 Jan 1973.

    ii. Hannah Margaret Judd. Born, 23 Feb 1977.

42. George Hannah[10] Elcan, III (George Hannah, 9). Born, 18 Sep 1952. He married Stephanie Leigh Beale, 14 Apr 1984, in Lynchburg,

VA. Born, 18 Oct 1958. Children:
   i. Adam Seth[11] Elcan. Born, 17 Jan 1985.
   ii. Sarah Catherine Elcan. Born, 9 Mar 1987.
   iii. Rebecca Margaret Elcan. Born, 16 Dec 1990.

43. Margaret Lee[10] Rosen. Born, 28 Aug 1947, in Farmville, VA. She married Glenn Spangler Bair. 24 Feb 1967. Children:
   i. Glenn Spangler[11] Bair, Jr. Born 7 Nov 1968, in Baltimore, MD.
   ii. William Alexander Bair. Born, 28 Mar 1972, in Baltimore, MD.

44. Carl Coleman[10] Rosen, Jr. Born, 31 Jul 1948. He married Susan Lynn Grier, 19 Aug 1972. Born, 19 Aug 1952, in Bel Air, MD. Children:
   i. Christopher Coleman[11] Rosen. Born, 16 Nov 1990, in Roanoke, VA.

45. Gary Russell (Russie)[10] Carden. Born, 27 Oct 1943, in New York, NY. She married John Louis Huber, 14 Aug 1965. Children:
   i. Heather Carden[11] Huber. Born, 9 Nov 1967, in Atlanta, GA.
   ii. Brian Campbell Huber. Born, 17 Apr 1970.

46. Gary Ann[10] Donaldson (Robert Walter, 9). Born, 8 Mar 1956, in Atlanta, GA. She married David G. Allen, 7 Jul 1976. Child:
   i. Travis James[11] Allen. Born, 26 Mar 1979.

47. Mary Robyn[10] Gilliam (John Robert, 9). Born, 28 Jul 1950, in Huntsville, AL. She married Thomas Buford Reed, III, 9 Aug 1975, in San Antonio, TX. Children:
   i. Matthew Jomas[11] Reed,. Born, 15 Oct 1977, in San Antonio, TX.
   ii. Delray June Reed,. Born, 4 Nov 1978, in San Antonio, TX.

48. Karen Kelly[10] Gilliam (Richard Holland, 9). Born, 5 Aug 1952, in Huntsville, AL. She married Randal Paul Andress, 21 Jan 1984, in Huntsville, AL. Children:
   i. John Richard[11] Andress. Born, 2 Jul 1985, in Huntsville, AL.
   ii. Kelly Carpentar Andress. Born, 12 Apr 1988, in Huntsville, AL.

NOTES AND REFERENCES

1. Miss Elsie W. Gilliam of Lynchburg, Virginia, in 1963, wrote Mrs. Richard Holland Gilliam, Jr., of Gurley, Alabama, the following: "Don't you remember the story I wrote you about Col. Richard Holland Gilliam's

last wife,(Hettie Williams? He was undoubtedly in love with her all the time. He courted her first but her step-mother had died and left a baby and she said she couldn't leave the baby. He married and after his first wife died he came back and courted Aunt Hettie again. She didn't think the child was old enough for her to leave and she refused again. He married the second time, and when that wife died he came back to Aunt Hattie. She thought the child was old enough for her to leave this time and she married him, but with this stipulation - if she died, he was to bring her back to Lynchburg for burial, "because there was no honor being buried in a country graveyard." She and all her family had a good sense of humor. He was good as his word. He died first and was buried in the Williams lot."

2. This was possibly his second marriage, first wife unknown.
3. Based on 1850 census.
4. Without issue.
5. Age 44 in 1850 census.
6. Age 21 in 1850 census.
7. Age 12 in 1860 census; born at Millcote.
8. or 14 Sep 1910.
9. or 29 June 1887.
10. They lived at "Millcote, " Buckingham, VA.

SOURCES OF INFORMATION ON THE GILLIAM FAMILY

1. The papers of Margaret Gilliam Strock, Charlotte, NC.
2. Richard Holland Gilliam Bible.
3. Glover-Gilliam Bible.
4. Gilliam Notes from St. Peter's Parish Register.
5. The papers and charts of Mrs. Richard H. Gilliam, Jr., Huntsville, AL.
6. The obituaries of the Richard Lee Gilliam Family, sent by Robert Walter Donaldson, Melbourne, FL.
7. Inscription on Col. Gilliam's grave, Spring Hill Cemetery, Lynchburg, VA, contributed by Anna B. Elcan.
8. The Holmans of Virginia by Harry Stuart Holman.
9. Souvenir pamphlet, "Landover," of the reunion of the Descendants of Dr. and Mrs. Glover Davenport Gilliam (1947). By Rosa M. Gilliam.

10. Richard Lee Gilliam family records, contributed by Mrs. Helen Preble Stewart, Bend, OR.
11. Notes on the Anderson family contributed by Mrs. Claudia Anderson Chisholm, Mineral, VA.

Sheriff receipt book and papers of Col. Richard H. Gilliam

Names have been spelled variously in the Gilliam Papers. These original spellings have not been altered. Thus we have variations such as Holman, Holeman, etc.

-A-

AARON, 25, 33

ABBITT,
  William Jones, 72

ABBOTT,
  Wyatt, 22

ABELL,
  George, 50
  Williams, 50

ABRAHAM, 61
  A.D., 10, 17, 30
  Anderson D., 30, 61

ADAMS, 2, 61
  Amanda Jones, 66
  Isaac, 2
  Jesse T., 71
  Richard E., 69

AGEE,
  James M., 50
  Thomas, 50
  Thomas W., 18, 23

AGGEY, 65

AGGY, 65

AGIE, 58

AKERS,
  Bryan, 33

ALFRED, 13

ALLEN, 20, 26, 27, 42, 55
  David G., 78
  Travis James, 78

ALVIS,
  William W., 11

AMANDA, 28, 58

AMHERST,
  Charles L., 40

AMOS,
  Frs., 47
  Judith, 42

ANDERSON, 57, 61
  Benjamin D., 41
  D., Jr., 16
  Dabney William, 70
  David, Jr., 13, 19
  Edgar, 70
  Edward Lawrence, 66, 70
  Eliza Ann, 70
  Elizabeth G., 33
  Garland, 54
  J.M., 55
  James, 4, 15, 20, 26, 65
  L., 26
  Laurence, 6, 15, 18, 20
  Lawrence, 6, 13, 50, 66
  Richard Alexander, 70
  S., 26
  Richard Lawrence, 70
  Virginia Elizabeth, 66

ANDRESS,
  John Richard, 78
  Kelly Carpentar, 78
  Randall Paul, 78

ANDREWS,
  Robert S., 53

ANICA, 31

ANNIE, 32

APPLING,
  R.C., 54

ARCHER, 31

AUSTIN,
  A., 1, 16, 18, 48
  Archer, 14, 16, 50
  Archibald, 1, 2, 14, 17, 20, 25, 50
  Bernard, 1, 16, 17
  Frances, 1
  George, 1
  Grace, 1
  Grace R., 1
  J.M., 19, 24, 25, 57
  James M., 1
  James, Jr., 40
  John, 1
  John, Dr., 24
  Martha E., 1
  T., 11
  Th., 25
  Thomas, 1, 2, 8, 10, 13, 14, 16, 18, 19, 20, 47, 48, 50

AYRES,
  Jane, 69

-B-

B...,
  Thomas, 50
  Thomas Andrew, 50

BABER,
  Brightbury G., 30

BAGLEY,
  George, 35
BAIR,
  Glenn Spangler, 78
  William Alexander,
  78
BAKER,
  Andrew, 53
  John B., 53
BALDWIN, 7
  A.A., 34
BALSER, 58
BARBARA, 57
BARBER, Mary, 73
BARNES,
  Annie Franklin, 73
BASKERVILLE,
  Mary, 50
BASS,
  D.O., 4
BATTEN,
  Carol, 73
BAYLEY,
  M.H., 25
  Madison H., 24
BEALE,
  Stephanie Leigh, 77
BECKLEY,
  Joseph, 50
BELL,
  Lillian, 71
  P.B., 50
BEN, 9, 11, 13, 21
BENTLY, 14
  E.B., 34
BETSY, 58
BIBB,
  George W., 4, 50

Henry, 4, 50
BILLY, 8, 13
BLACKWELL,
  Mayme Allen, 75
BLAND, 40
BLANTON,
  James, 16
BLUNDLE, 42
BOATRIGHT,
  Benjamin
BOATWRIGHT
  B., 41
  Betty, 41, 42
  D., 40
BOB, 57
BOCCOCK,
  W.P., 27
Willis P., 27
BOCK, 50, 52
BOCOCK, 28, 31
  Charles T., 35, 43
  J.H.S., 50
  J.T., 9, 15, 35, 50
  John T., 17, 58
  N.F., 35
  T.S., 50
  W.P., 24, 26, 34, 35,
  50
  Willis P., 35
BOLLING,
  Phillip A., 43
BOLLINGS, 50
BONDURANT, 28, 31
  David, 37
  John, 57
  T.M., 12
  Thomas M. 43
  William, 39

William F., 5, 6, 47
BOOKER, 9
  B.G., 13, 18
  Eloise Glover, 66
  Ethel, 72
  George, 4, 9, 10
  George Richard, 71
  H.T., 70
  Loulie Emma, 71
  Norman Courtney, 71
  R.A., 59
  Richard Edward, 70
  Richard Glover, 71
  Sallie Love, 70
  Walter T., 71
BOOTWRIGHT,
  Anne, 73
BOWMAN,
  Rev., Mr., 59
  Sallie, 72
BOWN,
  Joel G., 60
BRANCH, 2, 7, 10,
11, 13, 14, 20, 61
  Henry B., 16
  Sam, 13
  W., 31
  William, 2, 14, 19, 20
  Wilson, 50
BRAZELEY,
  Robert, 8
BRIGHTWELL, 2,
61
  Archibald R., 53
  Joseph, 2, 61
  Josiah W., 5
  Samuel, 44

William, 53
BROADAS,
 Reubin, 11
BROADUS,
 R., 16
BROWN, 50
 B., 58
 James, 5, 24, 27, 57, 61
 Joel G., 60, 61, 67
 John, 33
 John C., 46
 John D., 47
 L. G., 53
BROYLER, 71
 Daisy, 71
BRYAN,
 Wilson P., 2
BRYANT, 2, 8, 61
 John B., 50
 Martin, 41
 Tibereous, 35
BUCKS,
 Samuel, 47
BUDWELL,
 Leigh 72
BULLINGTON,
 D., 16, 17
BURKS,
 Joseph, 7, 50
 Samuel, 45
 Samuel L., 46
 William, 10
BURNETT,
 Anna Meade, 76
 Eddie Samuel, 76
 Thomas, 54

BURTEN,
 Robert, 40
BURTON, 9
BUSH,
 Mary, 69
BYREE,
 Martha, 73
 Octavia, 74

-C-
CABEL, 4
CABELL, 2
 Ben W.T., 4
 Benjamin W.S., 4
 C., 23
 Cavis W., 2
 Clifford, 2, 3, 4, 5, 6, 11, 33, 43, 50
 D. Clifford, 41
 E.W., 25, 47
 Edmund W., 6, 21
 Frd., 46
 Frederick M., 47
 Lewis W., 2, 3, 4, 5, 6, 27, 61
 T.M., 50
CALAHAM,
 Minnie, 71
CALEY, 13
CALLAHAN,
 John P., 4
CAMBELL, 25
CAMPBELL, 11
 James, 12
CARDEN,
 Russell Campbell, 76
 Gary Russell, 76, 78

CARNIFIX,
 Mary, 50
CARTER, 10
 Elizabeth, 72
 Jesse A., 39
 Silas, 72
 Thomas, 72
CASON,
 Fugua, 50
 H.B., 47
 Hiram B., 48
CASSON,
 James, 50
CELIA, 65
CHADWICK,
 Dora, 73
CHAMBERS,
 John W., 14, 18
 Willis, 13
CHARLES, 9, 22
CHARLIE, 65
CHARY, 58
CHEATWOOD, 7, 8, 9, 10, 11, 12, 20, 23, 51
CHEEDLE,
 J. R., 53
 J. T., 53
CHENAULT,
 John, 48
CHICK,
 J.A., 8
 James A., 8
 William, 50
CHILDER,
 Alfred, 62
CHILDERS,
 Alfred, 37

CHISHOLM,
  Claudia Anderson, 80
CHOCKLEY,
  A.D., 54
CHRISTIAN, 9
  Charles L., 8, 17, 40
  G., 20
  George, 3, 62
  James P., 34, 45
  Jonathan, 6
  Mary, 44
  Mary B., 44
  Rufus C., 35
  Samuel B., 41, 42
  Stephen, 14, 50
  Stephen W., 8
  W.D., 19, 39
  William, 50
  William D., 4, 5, 6, 15, 19, 20, 22, 39, 44
CHRYTIAN,
  Henry A., 8
CLAIBORUNE,
  Thomas O., 37
CLAIBOURNE,
  George W., 55
  Thomas O., 36
CLAY, 61
COBB,
  R.P., 16, 59
COBBS,
  Pleasant A., 39
  R.P., 11, 14, 16, 19
  Reubin P., 17
  Thomas, 40
  W.A., 18
  Watson B., 40

COKEE,
  William B., 37
COLEMAN, 6, 7
  C.D., 16
  Charles, 5, 7, 11
  Henry, 5
  Robert, 14, 19, 39
  William H., 32
CONER,
  William S., 56
CONNER,
  A., 11
  Abednego, 23
  Charles, 23, 50
  Elizabeth, 45
  James, 45
  John, 50
  William S., 33, 61
CONNERS,
  James, 48
COOD, 50
COOK,
  William B., 36
  William C., 71
COOKE,
  William B., 36
CORNISH,
  George D., 12
COX,
  Benjamin, 53
  Matthew A., 42
CRANK,
  James, 42
CREATED, 16
CRENSHAW,
  S.D., 59
CREWS,
  James, 48

CRIDDLE, 42
CRISTIAN,
  William D., 13
CROCKIN,
  Edwin J., 75
CROWES,
  Anna, 29
  John, 29
CROXTON,
  Samuel, 5
CULEY, 13
CUNNINGHAM,
  Samuel H., 53
CURD,
  Edward W., 37
CURL,
  George G., 3

-D-

DAN,
  John, 8
DANEL, 25
DANIEL, 65
DAVENPORT,
  Annie Slaughter, 71
DAVIDSON, 54
  Charles, 44
  Charles E., 57
  Erastus M., 29
  John, 50
  Judith, 50
  Lasamy, 29
  Luzany, 38
  Nace E., 38
  Stephen D., 39
DAVIS, 39, 55, 61
  James, 55
  James H., 17

John B., 53
Margaret, 53
Peter, 53
R.J., 56
W.D., 45
William Calvin, 74
DAVY, 9, 28
DEANE,
  James, 50
DELAWARE, 65
DEVENPORT,
  William W., 38
DIAL,
  Opal Lucille, 75
DICK, 25
DILLARD,
  Joseph S., 23, 50
DIUGUID,
  Fannie, 73
DOLPH, 24
DONALDSON,
  Dorothy Louise, 75, 76
  Edith Gary, 75, 76
  Gary Ann, 76, 78
  James William, 75
  Robert Walter, 75, 76 78, 79
DOSS, John, 50
DUGID,
  George S., 10, 14
DUNLOP,
  James, 3
DUNN,
  William J., 50
DURPHEY,
  Edward M.W., 6
DURPHY,
  E.M.W., 53

DUVAL,
  Philip, 6

-E-
EADY, 10
EAGLES,
  Jonas, 37
EAMONS,
  Virginia, 72
EANS ,
  Emeline, 44
EASTER, 21
EASTHER, 31
EDMONDS,
  Ruth Winstone, 76
EDMUND, 9
EDWARD, 58
EDWARDS, 42
ELCAN,
  Adam Seth, 78
  Anna B., 79
  Anne, 77
  Anne Burnett, 76
  George Hannah, 74, 75, 76, 77
  Henry Eugene, 75
  Lucy Irving, 75
  Marcus C., 74
  Margaret Adelaide, 75
  P.H., 57
  Patrick Henry, 57
  Rebecca Margaret, 78
  Ruth Virginia, 76
  Sarah Catherine, 78
  Virginia Estelle, 75, 76

William Cleveland, 75, 76
ELDRIDGE,
  Benjamin, 40
  R., 47, 59
  Rolfe, 65
ELICK, 24, 25
ELIZA, 24
ELLIS, 13
ENZWEILER,
  Ruth Kathrine, 77
EPPERSON,
  Martha Virginia, 66
EVANS, 50
  Augustus H., 71
  C. Edward, 71
  E.P., 56
  William, 33
  William M., 61

-F-
FALKNER,
  James M., 48
FANNY, 27
FANSS,
  James, 50
FARELEY,
  James H., 3
FARLEY,
  James H., 28
FARRIS,
  James, 50
FARROW,
  Charles, 53
FAYETTE, 10
FERGUSON, 2
  Bartlet, 50
  D., 46

D.H., 8, 12, 13, 19, 20
David, 60
David H., 48
H., 46
William, 8, 33
William G., 50
William U., 50
William W., 2, 7, 10, 11, 12, 13, 14, 15, 16, 17, 19, 20, 21, 61
William W.D., 50
FIELD, 8
FILLIS, 18
FILLMORE,
John Rollin, 77
Richard Millard, 76
FITZGERALD,
John, 44
FITZPATRICK,
Nicholas, 50
FIZJERALD,
John, 48
Joseph, 48
FLIPPEN,
Mary P. Hobson, 66
Mary Page, 67
Mary Page Hobson, 69
Thomas D., 67
FLOOD, 1, 3, 8, 9, 13, 14, 15, 17, 18, 19, 21, 26, 50, 61
H.D., 23, 50
Henry D., 3
J.W., 11, 50
John, 9
T.H., 50
Thomas H., 1, 3, 11, 15, 20, 26, 50

FLOURNEY,
William C., 61
FLOURNOY,
William C., 2
FLOYD, 58
FON,
James C., 16, 22
S., 22
FORBES, 7
Alexander, Jr., 34
Charlotte, 34
E.J.C., 34
James H., 6
Thomas, 21
W.W., 34
William W., 23, 41
FORD, 8, 11
Ambrose, 43
S., 12, 17
Samuel, 10, 14, 17, 19, 23
W.A., 73
FORE, 16
Samuel C., 53
FOSTER,
Fannie, 71
FRANCISCO,
P., 21
FRANK, 21
FRANKEY, 9
FRANKLIN, 8
FREDERICK, 19, 20
FRENCH,
J.H., 63
FRITWELL,
James B., 34
FURGUSON, 8

-G-
GARNETT, 61
A.C., 34
Thomas H., 34
William, 34
GARRET, 61
P.I., 61
GARRETT,
Wilson, 61
GARROTT,
Bashaba, 42
John, 18
Stephen, 42
GARVIN,
Mary Willie, 77
GARY, 35, 52, 60
Elizabeth Mary, 66, 69
J.B., 61
John, 5, 40, 66, 69
John B., 5, 59, 61, 66, 69
Lucy C., 61, 65
R.G., 56, 61
Richard G., 66, 69
Thomas, 65
GEORGE, 27, 28, 32, 65
GIBSON,
William F., 48
GILBERT, 66
Annie, 73
Cornelius, 72
Emma Josephine, 66
Emma Plunkett, 71
George, 72
George W., 72
Rosa Lee, 72

GILES,
 Benjamin, 54
 Josiah, 53
 Thomas, 53
GILLIAM, 55, 57, 58, 62, 78
 Amanda Jones, 69
 Ann E., 31, 32
 Ann Virginia, 66, 69
 Annie Eliza, 71
 Armistead Hamlet, 72
 Art. W., 25
 Benjamin Hobson, 66, 70
 Bettie Edmonia, 66, 68, 70
 Bobby, 73
 Charles, 58
 David, 73
 David Allen, 77
 David Michael, 73
 Dorothy Graham, 75, 76
 E.G., 34
 E.J., 5, 31, 33, 55, 64
 Edward, 45
 Edward Glover, 66, 69, 71
 Edward Holland, 73, 75
 Edward J., 31, 33, 41, 43, 54, 56, 61, 65, 66, 68, 70
 Eliza Bolling, 69, 71, 72
 Eliza G., 65
 Elizabeth, 65, 66
 Elizabeth Glover, 66, 67, 70

 Elizabeth Holland, 67
 Ella Coleman, 71
 Eloise Glover, 68
 Elsie W., 67, 78
 Elsie West, 73
 Emma Hubbard, 71
 Emma Josephine, 69, 72, 73
 Epaphroditus, 66, 67
 Fannie Diuguid, 73
 Fannie Jane, 71
 Floyd Herbert, 66, 70, 74, 75
 Frances Daniel, 73
 Georgia Williams, 74, 75
 Glover D., 65
 Glover Daniel, 66, 69
 Glover Davenport, 66, 68, 71, 72, 80
 Grace Schenk, 73
 Harriet E., 31
 Henry Eugene, 73, 75
 Isham, 58
 J.C., 32
 J.D., 32
 J.J., 58
 James Cornelius, 71
 James Richard, 66, 71
 James Thomas, 72
 Jane, 75
 John, 73
 John C., 31
 John D., 55, 56, 57, 61, 64
 John Floyd, 74, 75, 76, 77

 John H., 35
 John J., 29, 38, 59
 John Richard, 68, 71
 John Robert, 75, 77, 78
 John W., 32
 Karen Kelly, 77, 78
 Kristen Leigh, 77
 Lucy C., 66, 69
 Lucy Waller, 75
 Margaret, 66, 73
 Margaret Hannah, 75
 Margaret Virginia, 73, 74
 Marion, 66, 70, 73
 Marion W., 73
 Marion Williams, 73
 Mark Robert, 77
 Marshall Robertson, 73
 Martha Virginia, 68, 70
 Mary Jessie, 74
 Mary Marshall, 66, 69
 Mary P., 56
 Mary Robyn, 77, 78
 Mary Victoria, 66, 69
 Matthew Holman, 73
 Mattie Lee, 74
 Morning, 61
 Nancy, 66
 Olivia Ford, 69, 72
 Olivia West, 72
 Patricia Diane, 73
 Paul, 73
 Peggy, 73

R.H., Richard,
Richard H. - *This
names appears on vir-
tually every page in the
book.*

Richard Lee, 66, 69,
73, 75, 79

Robert Edward, 72

Robert L., 73

Robert Lawler, 74

Rosa M., 80

Rosa Maria, 72

Ruth Jane, 72

Sallie Virginia, 72

Sally W., 66, 69

Sandra Wall, 77

Stephen, 73

Terrence, 73

Thomas A., 73

Thomas Allen, 76

Thomas West, 66,
69, 73

Virginia, 31

Virginia Elizabeth,
66, 70

Walter Edward, 71

Walter Flood, 66,
69, 72

Walter Fuqua, 72

William, 65, 66, 68,
70

William Edward, 66,
69, 73, 74, 75

William Ernest, 74

William Herbert, 74

William Lee, 73

GILLISPIE,
William A., 18

GILLS,
Mary J., 44

GIPSON,
M., 43

Miles, 41

Polly, 51

GLOVER, 9, 33, 61

Davenport, 70

David W., 5, 22

E., 33

Edmund, 61, 66

Elizabeth, 51

Elizabeth A., 66

J., 18

J.B., 61

John, 22

John S., 22

Mary, 10

Robert, 5

S.A., 61

GODSAY,
Amanda, 42

GODSEY,
Lydia, 42

GOOCH, 8, 9, 10, 11,
12, 20, 51, 66

Charles, 73

Emma Josephine,
66, 73

John, 73

T., 7

GOODWIN,
James, 51

GORDEN,
Obadiah, 53

GORDON,
Lydia, 57

Obd., 51

GOUGH,
William, 40

GRAHAM,
Bessie, 75

GREGORY, 16, 37,
56

Ann, 37

Edmund, 37

S., 24

Samuel, 36, 45, 55

W. Samuel, 61

GRIER,
Susan Lynn, 78

GRIGGS,
Hardin, 29

James, 42

Mary, 29

GRUBB,
Sarah, 53

Thomas, 53

GUILL,
Nathaniel, 39

GURRANT,
D., 62

GUY, 14

-H-
HAMLET,
Jane Lewis, 72

HAMMER,
James A., 50

HAN, 21

HANCOCK, 2, 61

Ammon, 2

HANES,
Jane S., 10

HANNAH, 65

Laura Adelaide, 74

HARDAMAN,
Littlebury, 38

HARDEMAN,
  Bibzer, 38
HARDIMAN, 28
  Anderson, 29, 38
  Berry, 25, 38
  Charles, 23, 28, 30, 38, 39
  Charles G., 30, 31
  Charles S., 30
  Elizabeth, 29
  George, 50
  George H., 30
  George W., 31
  Harriett, 38
  J.B., 34
  John, 31, 34, 38
  John E., 29, 38
  John w., 39
  L.B., 30, 57
  Litelberry, 26
  Littlebarry, 34
  Littleberry, 28, 29, 30, 31, 55, 57
  Littlebury, 38
  S.B., 28
  Samuel, 29, 30, 31
  Samuel B., 50
  Samuel G., 30
  Susan, 29
  Thomas, 29, 38
  William, 29, 31, 38
  William J., 29
HARDIMON,
  Little Berry, 23
HARDWICK,
  S.P., 18, 21
  Samuel P., 5

HARDWICKE,
  S.P., 4
  Samuel P., 6, 55
HARDYMAN,
  Harriatt, 38
  Samuel, 38
HARIOTT,
  R.N., 32
HARRIS, 41
  C., 56
  Claibron, 53
  James, 12
  James M., 16
  Jane S., 12
  John, 50
  John M., 43
  Robert, 12
  William, 49
HARRISON, 65
HARRY, 58, 65
HARVEY,
  John H., 44
  Polley, 42
  William W., 64
HASKINS,
  John W., 40
HATCHER,
  Joseph, 67
  Josiah, 16
  Sally W., 67, 69
  Samuel, 5
  Virginia C., 66
  Virginia Catherine, 67
HENDRECK,
  G.W., 34
HENRY, 26, 58

HENRY,
  Annie Holmes, 72
HICKOK,
  P.H., 18
HILL,
  Heller, 56
  J., 18
  Tower, 58
HIX,
  Samuel, 54
  W., 8, 15
  William, 3
  Wilson, 3, 8, 11, 12, 13, 17, 19, 21, 22, 41, 51
HOBSON,
  Benjamin, 67, 69
  Mary Page, 67, 69
  Sally W., 67
HOCKER, 23
  George, 42
  Robert K., 42
HOLEMAN, 10, 14, 20, 41
  N.A., 44
  Nathan A., 41, 42
  Tandy, 29, 38
HOLLAND,
  Henry W., 53
HOLLIS,
  Patricia, 73
HOLMAN, 2, 61
  Harry Stuart, 79
  Jane Ayres, 67
  Tandy, 29, 59
  Virginia C., 66, 69
  William, 2, 67, 69
HOLMES,
  Elva, 74

HOOPER,
  Benjamin, 36
HORSLEY,
  John, 49, 50
HUBARD,
  E.W., 4
  R.T., 4
HUBER,
  Brian Campbell, 78
  Heather Carden, 78
  John L., 78
HUNDLEY,
  Elisha J., 4
  Juliet Jefferson, 75
  Lucy A., 49
HUNT, 26, 57
HURT,
  B., 24, 37
  Barnet, 24, 37
  Barnett, 24, 36
  Martin, 24, 36

-I-
INGLE,
  Anderson, 43
IRVING,
  H., 40
  Joseph, 40
  Joseph K., 1, 7
  R.K., 59
  Samuel R., 28
ISAAC, 11, 14, 65
ISBELL, 10, 52
  John W., 35
  Lewis D., 35, 51
  Thomas, 11
  Thomas U., 51

  Thomas W., 1, 3, 4,
  5, 6, 15, 17, 19, 20, 23,
  26, 34, 35
  W., 23
  William, 1, 3, 4, 5, 6,
  11, 19, 20
  ISHAM, 15, 26

-J-
JACK, 25, 58, 65
JACKSON,
  Patrick H., 17
JACOB, 13
JAMES, 65
  Wadworth, 22
JANE, 58
JENNINGS,
  Benjamin W., 51
  Bint., 51
  Jesse, 51
JIM, 13, 14, 17, 21
JINNY, 57
JOE, 13, 15, 20, 21,
  26, 27, 65
JOHN, 9, 13, 22, 58
JOHNS,
  John, 14, 19, 47
  Thomas, 22
JOHNSON,
  David, 1
  Genl. M., 10
  George M., 61
  Henry R., 54
  Jessie Belfield, 71
  John, 51
  John H., 12, 28, 51
  Miland, 12
  P., 14
  Peter, 11

  Richard, 51
  Richard, Sr., 51
  Thomas, 51
  Washington, 51
JOLLEY,
  James Elton, 77
JONATHAN, 47
JONES,
  A.R., 18
  C.J., 12
  Cinncinnatus F., 4
  D.C., 47
  David C., 6
  Eliza B., 66
  Eliza Bolling, 68
  Elizabeth, 51
  James, 22
  Josias, 51
  L.D., 61
  N.W., 61
  Paschal, 43
  Paul, 14
  Powhatan, 34
  S., 31
  Sam, 9
  Spotswood, 31
  W.B., 51
  W.D., 36, 37
  William B., 51
  William D., 15, 33, 61
JORDEN,
  Alfred, 44
JORDIN, 22
JUDD,
  David Cyrus, 77
  Elizabeth Burnett, 77
  Hannah Margaret,
  77

JUDY, 65

-K-
KATEY, 16
KATY, 10, 11
KELLER,
Emma Walton, 70
KELLY,
Catherine Russell, 77
KENT,
J.W., 72
KICHIN,
William A., 14
KING, 24
Alfred, 54
KITCHEN,
Aren, 11
Creed, 23
William A., 10, 11
KITCHIN,
Creed, 49
E., 49
Elijah, 49
John H., 49
William, 51
William A., 7, 51
William B., 49
KNAP,
Fred W., 18
KNIGHT,
Floyd, 73
KUYKENDALL,
Nathaniel White, 70
KYLE,
David, 40, 41, 42
G.W., 36
George W., 11, 62
H.C., 12, 51

-L-
LACKLAND, 57
James, 34
LACY,
George Hamilton, 75
LANCASTER,
John A., 41, 42
William L., 31
LAND,
A., 46
Frances, 46
Francis, 46
Thomas C., 32
LAWLER,
Bobbie Lee, 74
Mary, 73
Mollie, 73
William, 73
William Jesse, 74
LAWSON,
Elizabeth, 66
Epaphroditus, 66
Margaret, 66
LAYNE,
Gabriel, 49
Samuel S., 2, 51
LEGON,
H.A., 39
LEITCH,
William, 18
LEWIS, 42
Codelia, 70
Isaih, 53
M., 43
Shadreck, 70
Tarlton P., 55
Virginia, 70

LIFFORD,
Amos, 53
LIGHTFOOT,
John, 40
LIGON,
J.T., 57
Joseph T., 24, 25
LINTHICUM, 7, 9
C., 51
Edward, 51
Henry, 9, 51
John T., 53
LIPPORD,
John, 53
LIPSCOMB,
W., 60
William, 34
LONG,
Armstead, 3
Elizabeth H., 3
LOUISIA, 65
LOVERN,
Anderson J., 53
P.H., 7
LUBAN,
S.S., 59
LUCY, 23, 65

-M-
McCANCE,
Thomas W., 3
McCRAW,
Cary H., 43
Charles Dancy, 70
Edward Cary, 70
Lucy Lee, 70
Mary Emma, 70
Richard Miller, 70

William Emmett, 66, 70

McDEARMON,
Samuel D., 5

McDEASMON,
Samuel, 47

McFADDEN,
Francis, 45
Sally, 28, 49
William, 28

McFADDIN,
Francis, 28
Sally, 28

McFADEN,
Jer., 51

McFADIN,
Jer.tus , 51
Martha, 51
William, 51

McGLASSON,
Marcus P., 53

McKENNEY,
Charles, 37

McKENNY, 18

McKINEY,
Charles, 17

McKINNEY, 61
Charles, 21
George W., 42
Thomas, 54

McKINY,
Charles, 53

McNEED,
Johnson, 53

MADDOX,
Anna, 30
Josiah, 30

MAHALA, 65

MARIA, 21

MARTHA, 24, 65

MARTIN,
James, 53

MARY, 8, 13

MAT, 65

MATHEWS, 9
F., 53
George H., 31
Margaret Daniel, 73
S., 53
Sarah, 56
Tarlton, 53
W.H., 10, 12, 19
William Daniel, 73
William H., 11, 12, 13, 14, 16, 18, 46

MATTHEWS, 9
George H., 6
John, 39, 51
Tandy, 39
William H., 7, 9, 10, 14, 48, 51
William Thomas, 10

MATTOX,
Anna, 29

MAXEY,
A., 43
Charles L., 23
Martha, 23
Ouesby, 23

MEEM,
John G., 4

MEGGERSON,
Archibald B., 47
S.B., 45

MEGGINSON,
A.B., 11, 16

Archibald B., 39
John, 51
Joseph, 51
Joseph C., 51
Samuel B., 12, 47, 51
Samuel b., 46
Thomas, 32
William, 11, 17
William W., 51

MEGLEYNO,
Paschal F., 33

MELTON, 71
Eliza Bolling, 71

MEREDITH, 63
J.W., 28, 63
James, 62
James P., 68

MERIDETH,
Henry T., 45
James, 45

MERRYMAN,
Ralph, 53
Thomas H., 64

MICKLE,
Joel E., 53

MIKE, 65

MILES,
Charles, 51

MILEY, 24

MILLER, 7
Edward B., 17
Lewis t., 28
Thomas, 54
William, 17, 26
William A., 19

MILLY, 28

MIX,
Daniel P., 71

MONCUN,
Dunlop, 22
MONCUNE,
Henry, 3
MONCURE, 3
MONROE, 65
MOON,
William J., 53
MOORE, 7
Benjamin A., 51
Obadiah, 11, 18
Robert, 5, 6, 13, 18, 39, 51
Sarah, 54
William, 51
MOORIS,
B., 50
MORGAN, 61
J.P., 18, 23
John, 23, 25, 32, 34, 35
John P., 6, 18, 21
Joseph E., 1
MORRIS, 4
B.T., 3
Benjamin, 46
Benjamin H., 39
Benjamin S., 2, 3, 5, 6, 47, 61
John, 17, 18, 19, 21, 23, 28, 29, 33, 35, 38, 40, 41, 46, 58, 62
John James, 19
N.D., 5
Nathaniel, 35, 36, 37, 41
R.G., 46, 50, 51
Samuel, 5, 35

MORTON,
Charles A., 3, 61
Thomas S., 3, 61
MOSBY,
John W., 1, 6
MOSELEY, 7, 15, 18, 23, 61, 62
A., 58
Alex., 32, 58
Alexander, 43
Arthur, 58, 59
Benjamin, 3
C.F., 58
Charles F., 58
E.B., 2, 21
Edward B., 2
G.B., 33
Gr., 51
Grandison, 29, 38
J., 2, 16, 21, 33
Joseph, 2
Josiah, 9, 24, 61, 62, 63
R.E., 51
Robert E., 51
Va. R., 51
W.C., 9
William, 43, 51
William B., 9
William C., 17
William M., 1, 28, 35, 63
William P., 51, 58
William W., 9
MOSELY,
William M., 10, 53
MOSES,
Bessie, 72

MOSLEY,
Josiah, 53
Thomas, 53
MUNSON, 43
MURFEY,
Daniel, 36, 37

-N-
NANCY, 8, 22, 65
NATUS, 11
NEAL, Sharry Lynn, 77
NED, 8, 27
NEIGHBOURS,
James E., 66, 69
Sally W., 25, 65
W., 25
Wilborn, 66, 69
NELSON, 8, 11, 12, 13, 31
NEWTON,
John, 41
NICHOLAS, 23, 41
NICY, 21, 22
NORTH,
Anthony, 51
Anthony A., 51
Charles, 51
NOWLIN, 1, 13, 15, 19, 26, 50, 61
Bryant, 1, 51
NUNNALLY, 7
Granville, 9

-O-
OAKES,
Jamor, 51
OBRIANT,
M.C., 5

OLIVER,
  Francis, 42
  Lucy C., 66
  William, 66, 69
  William P., 16, 18
OLIVERS,
  William P., 41
OVERTON,
  James W., 51
OVETIN, 40

-P-
PAGE, 25
PALMER, 52
  R.D., 9, 52
PALMORE,
  Joseph, 52
PAMPLIN,
  J., 7
  James, 15
  P., 7
  Patrick, 39
PANKEY,
  James, 14, 51
  John, 14, 52
  Peter B., 52
  S., 7
  Stephen, 23
PAROCK,
  S.H., 16
  Thomas, 19
PARRACK,
  Thomas, 45, 55
  William H., 5
PATTESON, 39, 42
  Benjamin, 9
  James, 51
  John S., 44

Judeth B., 49
R.B., 68
Robert B., 13
S.D., 14
Turner H., 34, 44, 45
William, 19, 21
PATTISON,
  Benjamin, 51
  Charles, 6
  James M., 43
  Robert, 51
  Turner H., 51
  William, 51, 52
PAYNE,
  G. M., 9
  George M., 17
  T.D., 75
PENY, 24
PERKINS,
  Catharine M., 59
  H., 19
  Thomas F., 59
  Thomas H., 40, 54
  Thomas T., 52
  W.H., 52
PERKINSON,
  John P., 55
PERRY,
  Elizabeth R., 3
PETER, 15, 20, 26, 27
PETERS, 2, 27, 61
  Donald P.C., 5
  Frederick, 27
  Frederick G., 2, 21
PETTECREW,
  Matthew, 52
  William, 52

PETTESON,
  John, 24
PHAUP, 42
PHEBE, 30
PHELPS, 7, 8
  Alexander, 52
  Anna, 51
  C., 11
  Charles, 4, 19
  Elizabeth, 15
  J., 23
  J.P., 11, 14, 51
  James, 21, 51, 52
  John, 20
  John P., 19
  Jon. P., 52
  Jona. P., 9
  Jonathan P., 14
  Joseph, 51
  Mary, 18
  Mary S., 13, 19
  Nelson, 51
  P., 47
  Peter W., 51
  R.P., 8
  Richard, 10
  Robert, 9, 15, 51
  Robert A., 41
  Robert P., 8, 19, 52
  W.J., 52
  William E., 52
PHILLIPS, 58
PHILLIS, 23
PHILPS,
  J.P., 11
PITTMAN,
  James, 5
  John, 17, 19

John P., 48, 49
T.H., 27
Thomas, 62, 68
PLEASANT, 13
PLUNKET,
A., 23
Ambrose, 52
W.H., 23
POCAHONTAS, 68
PORTER,
William H., 53
POWELL, 65
PREBLE,
Eugene Wilford, 76
Helen Elizabeth, 76
PRICE,
Daisy, 71
Eliza Bolling, 66, 71
Martha, 54
Morton, 71
Motie, 71
Nathaniel, 71
Pugh, 53
Richard, 71
Thomas West, 71
Warner W., 2
William Jones, 71
PRYOR,
Benister S., 53
David, 47
William T., 49
PUGH,
Thomas, 12
PYLE,
George T., 33

-R-
RACHEL, 65

RAGLAND,
Richard, 49
RAINE,
Charles, 14
Hugh, 14, 23
Richard K., 12
RAKES,
Ann, 49
Benjamin, 49
Elizabeth, 49
Henry, 49
John, 49
William, 48
RAMSEY,
Anna Steel, 72
RANDOLPH, 28, 30
RANSONE,
John, 53
RATCLIFFE,
James M., 3
REED,
Delray June, 78
Matthew Jomas, 78
Thomas Buford, 78
REES,
Edward, 42
REVES, 52
REYNOLDS,
Frances, 24
Francis, 52
Frs., 25
Isaac, 52
Isaac R., 22
M., 37
Ola, 72
Sophia Jane, 24
RHODA, 65
RICHARDSON,

Richard P., 53
RICKARDSON,
Tample D., 3
RIVES, 9
Robert, 2, 61
ROBERT, 30
S.E., 43
ROBERTS,
Waddy W., 3
Zachariah, 3
ROBERTSON,
Blanche, 72
Elizabeth, 38
Hugh, 43
J.S., 5
William H., 38
ROBINSON,
Hugh D., 52
James, 52
Windslow, 12
Woodie Rae, 77
ROLERSON, 28
ROLFE,
John, 68
Pocahontas, 68
ROSEN,
Carl Coleman, 76, 78
Christopher
Coleman, 78
Margaret Lee, 76, 78
ROUTON,
John, 36
ROWTON,
John H., 65
ROZANA, 65
RUSH,
G., 12
George, 41, 55

RYAN,
  Charles J., 6

-S-
SALLE,
  Isaac, 52
SALLY, 17, 32
SAM, 24, 57, 65
SANDERS,
  Goodrick, 37
  Thomas, 65
SANDERSON,
  Eva, 72
SARAH, 58
SAUNDERS,
  Francis, 27
  G.D., 18
  R., 44
  Zenas, 36
SAYNE,
  Samuel s., 61
SCOTT, 61
  Kitty, 42
  Rhoda, 42
SCRUGGS, 9
  E.L., 9
  Ed. S., 10
  Frederick, 43
SEA..?,
  Coleman, 52
SELVY, 21
SETH, 65
SHACKLEFORD,
  John, 16
  John C., 17
SHAPARD,
  John, 72

SHAW,
  R., 9
  Robert, 11, 12, 34
SHEPPARD, 16
  William B., 16
SHORE,
  W.P., 34
SHRAP,
  Frederick W., 16
SIMMONS,
  Joel, 14
  Mae, 74
SIMS,
  P.O., 59
SIPE,
  Peter, 56
SISAN,
  J.H., 44
SLAZEY, 58
SMITH, 9
  Charles, 46, 47, 49
  J.T., 22
  James T., 1, 6, 9
  Jane, 72
  Judith, 29, 38
  Russell M., 62
  Samuel, 29, 38
SNELL,
  Begin, 53
SNILLING, 24
SOPHIA, 65
SPELLER,
  G.A., 18
  J., 18
  S.F., 16, 17
  Samuel F., 19
SPENCER, 15, 28, 61
  David, 10

John, 44
John R., 52
Lot, 10
Lott, 23, 27
Moseley, 18, 22, 23
Moses A., 29, 38, 59
Nathan, 2, 10
William, 23, 52
William G., 57
William J., 57
SPENSER,
  Moseley, 18
SPILLER,
  Preston H., 61
  Preston Henry, 69
SPROUSE, 42
  Roland, 42
STAINBACK,
  A.E., 56
STALKUM,
  James, 52
STAPLES, 52
STEGAR,
  J.A., 61
  S.B., 61
STEGER,
  Edwin, 59
STELL,
  William, 52
  William H., 52
STEPHANS,
  James C., 3
STEPHEN, 13, 22, 65
STEPHENS,
  Absalom, 52
  James C., 3
STERN,
  H., 56

STEWART,
Alan Crawford, 76
Helen Preble, 80
STINSON,
George, 52
John, 39, 44, 52
STRATTON,
Abraham, 48
Asa, 16
STROCK,
Howard, 75
Margaret Gilliam, 79
STUART,
James W., 24
SUCKEY, 30, 31
SUCKIE, 58
SUKEY, 25
SWENEY,
Daniel, 12
SWOOPE,
William M., 57

-T-
TALBOT,
Nancy, 28, 66
TALBOTT,
Nancy, 68
TALLEY,
John P., 15
TALLY,
J.P., 15
TAPSCOTT,
Jonas M., 16
TAYLOR,
A.H., 52
Jackquelin, 21
William Coleman, 75
William D., 54

THACKSTON,
Henry C., 31, 32
William W., 53
THOMAS,
Charles, 19, 52
THOMPSON,
John Jr., 1, 7
THORNHILL,
Elizabeth, 52
Nelson, 22
Sally, 12, 19, 22
Thomas W., 8, 11,
12, 15
William, 17
William, Jr., 52
THORNTON, 62
Frs., 61
N.H., 17
Nathan H., 19, 33,
35, 58
W.H., 40
THURMAN,
Marshall P., 28
THURMOND,
William D., 6
William K., 1
William M., 1, 9, 17,
22
TICE,
James R., 73
John P., 73
Pamela E., 73
TIDMORE,
Robert Nathan, 77
TINDALL,
Edmdund, 39
William M., 9
TINDELL,
John, 40

TOM, 11, 26, 28, 31
TOPP,
William, 37
TRENT, 3, 8, 14, 17,
18, 21, 23, 50
John, 52
John C., 16
Thomas, 3, 15, 19,
20, 21, 22, 23, 26, 52
TURNER,
Jefferson D., 5
Russie, 72
TWYMAN,
J.L., 58
TYLER,
Charles, 52
Elizabeth, 29, 38, 55
Lawson, 29, 30, 55
Lawson G., 2, 29, 38
TYNES,
Colie, 71

-V-
VAWTER, 8
S.P., 8, 10, 20
Silas P., 3, 10, 22
VENABLE,
A., 17
VEST,
Benjamin, 49
Samuel, 49
VIER,
James, 32
VIRGIN,
Mary Elizabeth, 76

-W-
WACKENS,

Phil, 52
WACKER,
  S.J., 51
WADE, 48
  George, 48
  John, 22
  John R., 3, 28
  Nancy, 48
  William, 48
WALDEN,
  H.A., 25
WALKER, 11, 24
  Ben, 52
  Ben P., 52
  David, 53
  F.N., 59
  Gabriel, 52
  J.J., 23, 25
  S.J., 9, 12, 13
  Sam, 53
  Samuel, 21
  Samuel J., 4, 5, 10,
11, 12, 35, 47, 52
  T.J., 8
WALL,
  James, 52
WALTON, 7
  James C., 6
  William, 11, 47
WARRINER,
  David, 52
  William, 37
WATKINS, 50
  Edward, 53
  F.N., 2
  H.P., 52
  Jason, 53
  Joel, 22, 33, 52

P.A., 17
  Perry, 53
  Philip, 2, 14, 17, 18,
53
  Rhoda, 53
  S.J., 47
  Silas, 21
  Susan, 53
WATSON,
  Abner, 53
  Daniel P., 9, 28
  George E., 17
  James, 52
WATTS,
  Elizabeth Bowcock,
70
  J., 16
WEBB,
  Abram M., 52
  George, 2, 53
  James M., 2
  John, 21
  Levi, 18
  Martin, 52
  Merry, 52, 53
  William, 52
WEEKS,
  Iturea Elizabeth, 76
WELLS, 61
WERT,
  J.L., 61
WEST,
  Benjamin, 40
  John N., 4
  John S., 41
WHEELER,
  A., 14
  Andrew S., 11

WHIRLEY,
  Joshua, 54
WHITE, 9, 52
  And., 52
  Andrew, 52
WHITEHEAD,
  Mary, 34, 56, 61
WHITLER,
  Mourning, 42, 43
WHITLOW,
  Martin, 72
WILKERSON,
  James B., 39
  Nathaniel, 53
  Robert, 53
WILKINSON,
  G.E., 8
  George E., 10
WILLIAM, 13, 21
WILLIAMS, 7, 42
  Hettie, 70, 79
  Hettie Row, 66, 67,
70
  Jehu, 70
  John R., 44
WILLIE, 57, 58
WILLIS, 27
  Willis H., 27
WILLS, 2
  John W., 12, 19
  Willis H., 2
WILSON, 22, 58
  J.H., 53
  Joseph, 53
  W., 53
WIMBUSH,
  Abram W., 13

WINFIELD,
Thomas, 15
WINGFIELD, 7
E., 33
Eliza, 32
Lewis, 33
Lewis H., 32
Matthew, 52
Sophia Jane, 24
Thomas, 7, 24, 52
William A., 24
WINSTON, 72
Lillian, 72
WISE,
William S., 56, 61
WOOD,
C., 53
WOODBRIDGE,
Sawney, 28
WOODFIN,
James, 43
WOODING,
Alice, 72
Eliza Gilliam, 72
Ella Wilcox, 72
Emma, 72
James Richard, 72
Lillian, 72
Loulie M., 72
Martha Susan, 72
Nathaniel, 72
Olivia Ford, 66
Robert H., 72
Samuel Josiah, 72
Thomas H., 72
Thomas W., 72
West Gilliam, 72
Willie Hill, 72

WOODRIDGE,
S., 26
WOODROOF, 52
WOODSON,
Charles, 54
Drury, 52
Richard, 53
Tarlton, 52
WOODY,
Allen, 45
WOOTON,
Thomas B., 3
WORD, 55
Benjamin, 39, 40
Quin M., 43
Quinn M., 1, 61
Thomas, 17
W.C., 61
William H., 1, 13, 61
WRIGHT, 10, 37
David, 52
John M., 18, 52
Mary, 5, 6
Samuel, 36, 37
Samuel W., 24
T.P., 10
Thomas, 13, 18, 23, 52
Thomas F., 39
Thomas P., 11, 52
William, 52
William W., 41

-Y-
YANCY, 7
YOUNG, 2, 61
William T., 2
YOUNGER,

Edward F., 73

-Z-
ZAC, 33

www.ingramcontent.com/pod-product-compliance
Lightning Source LLC
Chambersburg PA
CBHW070255290326
41930CB00041B/2554